THEMATIC UNIT
Community Workers

Written by
Darlene Hardwick and Debbie Thompson

Teacher Created Materials, Inc.

P.O. Box 1040

Huntington Beach, CA 92647

©*1995 Teacher Created Materials, Inc.*

Made in U.S.A.

ISBN-1-55734-253-9

Illustrated by Jose L. Tapia

Edited by Janet Cain

Poems by Kathleen "Casey" Null

Cover Art by Theresa M. Wright

Table of Contents

Introduction

Community Workers contains a captivating whole language unit that is divided into four parts: People Who Build Our Homes, People Who Help Us Learn, People Who Keep Us Safe, and People Who Help Us Stay Healthy. Its 80 exciting pages are filled with a wide variety of lesson ideas and activities designed for use at the early childhood level. At its core are four high-quality children's literature selections, *Building a House, The Best Teacher in the World, Police,* and *Rita Goes to the Hospital.* For each of these featured books, activities are included which set the stage for reading, encourage the enjoyment of the book, and extend the concepts gained. In addition, the theme is connected to the curriculum with activities in language arts (including language experience and writing suggestions), math, science, social studies, art, music, and life skills (cooking, physical education, etc.). Many of these activities encourage cooperative learning. Suggestions and patterns for bulletin boards are additional time savers for the busy teacher. Furthermore, directions for student-created Big Books and culminating activities, which allow students to synthesize their knowledge in order to create products that can be shared beyond the classroom, highlight this very complete teacher resource.

This thematic unit includes:

❑ **literature selections**—summaries of children's books with related lessons (complete with reproducible pages) that cross the curriculum

❑ **poetry**—suggested selections and lessons

❑ **language experience and writing ideas**—suggestions as well as activities across the curriculum, including Big Books

❑ **bulletin board ideas**—suggestions and plans for student-created and/or interactive bulletin boards

❑ **homework suggestions**—extending the unit to the child's home

❑ **curriculum connections**—in language arts, math, science, social studies, art, music, and life skills (such as cooking and physical education)

❑ **group projects**—to foster cooperative learning

❑ **culminating activities**—which require students to synthesize their learning to create a product or engage in an activity that can be shared with others

To keep this valuable resource intact so it can be used year after year, you may wish to punch holes in the pages and store them in a three-ring binder.

Introduction *(cont.)*

Why Whole Language?

A whole language approach involves students in using all modes of communication: reading, writing, listening, observing, illustrating, experiencing, and doing. Communication skills are interconnected and integrated into lessons that emphasize the whole of language rather than isolating its parts. The lessons revolve around selected literature. Reading is not taught as a subject separate from writing and spelling, for example. A child reads, writes (spelling appropriately for his/her level), speaks, listens, etc., in response to a literature experience introduced by the teacher. In this way, language skills grow naturally, stimulated by involvement and interest in the topic at hand.

Why Thematic Planning?

One very useful tool for implementing an integrated whole language program is thematic planning. By choosing a theme with correlating literature selections for a unit of study, a teacher can plan activities throughout the day that lead to a cohesive, in-depth study of the topic. Students will be practicing and applying their skills in meaningful contexts. Consequently, they will tend to learn and retain more. Both teachers and students will be freed from a day that is broken into unrelated segments of isolated drill and practice.

Why Cooperative Learning?

Besides academic skills and content, students need to learn social skills. No longer can this area of development be taken for granted. Students must learn to work cooperatively in groups in order to function well in modern society. Group activities should be a regular part of school life, and teachers should consciously include social objectives as well as academic objectives in their planning. For example, a group working together to write a report may need to select a leader. The teacher should make clear to students and monitor the qualities of good leader-follower group interaction just as he/she would state and monitor the academic goals of the project.

Why Big Books?

An excellent cooperative, whole language activity is the production of Big Books. Groups of students or whole class can apply their language skills, content knowledge, and creativity to produce Big Books that can become part of the classroom library to be read and reread. These books make excellent culminating projects for sharing beyond the classroom with parents, librarians, other classes, etc. Big Books can be produced in many ways, and this thematic unit book includes directions for at least one method you may choose.

Learning Centers

Learning centers broaden and extend students' learning and understanding of the unit. Several types of centers are suggested below. You should adapt these ideas to fit your own classroom situation.

Storytime Center

This center gives students a place to sit comfortably as they listen to and discuss the story being read aloud. You may wish to provide a variety of carpet squares or pillows for students to use.

Book Center

This center is used to display books related to the unit. See the bibliography (pages 79-80) for suggestions.

Building Center

This center should be used when students are learning about People Who Build Our Homes (pages 6-34). Provide a variety of large and small blocks for students to use to build different types of homes. Display pictures of community workers who help build homes, such as bricklayers, carpenters, plumbers, electricians, painters, and equipment operators. You may also wish to display pictures of different types of homes from around the world.

Activity Center

This center can be used for many different purposes. It can include file folder activities, manipulatives, puzzles, and curriculum-related activities. Specific activities are described throughout this unit. Some activities should be completed with teacher direction, while others can be done independently.

Creative Role-Play Center

This center is used to enhance students' learning about community workers through dramatic play. Provide different types of clothing (hard hats, carpenter's apron, painter's cap, work gloves, doctor's white coat, surgeon's mask, firefighter's helmet, police officer's hat, etc.), and toys (dump truck, cement mixer, bulldozer, backhoe, tools, fire truck, police car, ambulance, school bus, doctor's kit, etc.) for students to use when role-playing the stories or during independent playtime.

Art Center

This center is where students create the art projects for this unit. Provide the art supplies that students will need to complete each activity. The tables should be covered with butcher paper, making them easier to clean.

Listening Center

This center gives students the opportunity to listen to and sing songs about community workers. See the bibliography (page 80) for suggestions.

Building a House

by Byron Barton

Summary

This book has colorful illustrations and a text that is easy for students to understand. It shows the process of how a house is built. Students will learn about the people whose job it is to help build houses, such as equipment operators, carpenters, plumbers, bricklayers, electricians, and painters. They will realize that all of these people must work together in order for a house to be built.

Suggested Activities

SETTING THE STAGE

1. Allow students to preview the book by reading aloud the title and showing them the pictures. Ask them what they think the book will be about.

2. Create different centers related to house building for students to use (page 5).

3. Display the bulletin board for People Who Help Build Our Homes (page 32).

4. Allow students to dig holes with toy equipment and/or real shovels.

5. Ask students if they have ever seen a house being built. Invite them to share what they know about the different jobs that are needed to build a house.

6. Encourage students to describe what their houses look like. Have them draw pictures of their homes (page 13).

7. Show different types of building and decorating materials, such as bricks, tiles, carpet squares, wood, shingles, and wallpaper and paint samples. Ask students to name each item that you show. Have students examine the materials. Encourage them to describe how the materials look and feel and how they would be used in building a house.

8. Display a variety of real tools. Discuss the purpose of each tool. Stress safety rules for handling tools. You may wish to post the safety rules.

9. Tell students about the history of tools. Point out that people have been using tools to build things since prehistoric times.

10. Have students cut out pictures of different types of homes from magazines and newspapers. Create a bulletin board collage by gluing the pictures onto butcher paper.

11. Take students on a walk around the school. Ask them to identify the names of different materials that were used to build the school, such as bricks, wood, and tile. Ask students how they think builders make those materials stay together. Lead students to conclude that builders must use nails, screws, glue, mortar, etc.

12. Show students pictures of homes from around the world. Help students understand how climate, available natural resources, and people's needs affect the kinds of homes that are built.

Suggested Activities *(cont.)*

ENJOYING THE BOOK

1. As you read the book, have students role-play different scenes. Discuss the pictures and the text. Ask students to identify different colors and shapes in the pictures.

2. Discuss the different people it takes to build a house and the importance of each career.

3. Ask students if they would like to work at any of the jobs described in the book. Make a career graph showing how many students would like to have each career. Ask students to interpret the graph by asking questions about it.

4. Have students sing the song shown below as you display the flannel pieces (pages 9-10). Have them use their hands to perform the actions described in the song.

This Is the Way We Build a House
(Sing to the tune of "The Farmer in the Dell")

There is a green, green hill.
There is a green, green hill.
Hi, Ho, now it is so,
There is a green, green hill.

Machines dig the hole.
Machines dig the hole.
Hi, Ho, now don't we know,
Machines dig the hole.

Builders hammer and saw.
Builders hammer and saw.
Hi, Ho, now hear them go,
Builders hammer and saw.

Next (or now) cement is poured.
Next, cement is poured.
Hi, Ho now watch it flow,
Next cement is poured.

Now workers lay the blocks.
Now workers lay the blocks.
Hi, Ho now watch them go,
Now workers lay the blocks.

It's time to make the floors.
It's time to make the floors.
Hi, Ho, they're way down low,
It's time to make the floors.

The walls will go up next.
The walls will go up next.
Hi, Ho, now up they go,
The walls will go up next.

The workers build a roof.
The workers build a roof.
Hi, Ho, now don't we know,
The workers build a roof.

The chimney's made from bricks.
The chimney's made from bricks.
Hi, Ho, the fire will glow,
The chimney's made from bricks.

The plumber puts in pipes.
The plumber puts in pipes.
Hi, Ho, the water flows,
The plumber puts in pipes.

The wires are now put in.
The wires are now put in.
Hi, Ho, the lights will glow,
The wires are now put in.

The windows go in next.
The windows go in next.
Hi, Ho, the air will flow,
The windows go in next.

The doors are put in place.
The doors are put in place.
Hi, Ho, they fit just so,
The doors are put in place.

The painters paint the house.
The painters paint the house.
Hi, Ho, the paint will flow,
The painters paint the house.

Then all the workers leave.
Then all the workers leave.
Hi, Ho, so there they go,
Then all the workers leave.

And now the house is built.
And now the house is built.
Hi, Ho, now we all know,
How a house is built.

Suggested Activities *(cont.)*

EXTENDING THE BOOK

1. Read aloud other books related to house building. See the bibliography (pages 79-80) for suggestions.

2. Assist students as they make filmstrips about building a house (pages 11-12).

3. Have students match pictures of tools with their outlines (pages 14-15).

4. Glue pictures of tools from magazines, newspapers, and catalogues onto index cards. Show students how to play Concentration matching types of tools, such as two hammers, two screwdrivers, two saws, etc. You may also wish to have students use the cards to group the tools into categories by what types of tools they are or by their functions.

5. On the chalkboard, write the names for different types of homes, such as a one-story house, two-story house, apartment, condominium, townhouse, farmhouse, ranch house, and duplex. Ask students in which kind of home they live. Use the information to create a graph. Have students interpret the graph by asking questions. Suggested questions: *How many students live in each type of home? Do more students live in duplexes or apartments? Where do the greatest number of students live? Where do the fewest live? What is the total number of students who live in one- and two-story homes?*

6. Present information about what an equipment operator does (page 16).

7. Follow the directions to prepare the Equipment Operator Puzzle for students (page 17). Show students how to put the puzzle together. Place the puzzles in reclosable plastic bags or envelopes. Encourage students to take their puzzles home to share with their families.

8. Use the activities to show what a bricklayer does (page 18).

9. Focus on the kinds of jobs that a carpenter does when a house is being built (page 19).

10. Help students make hard hats (pages 19-20).

11. Have students complete the activities to learn about plumbers (page 21), electricians (page 22), and painters (page 23).

12. Play a game called Who Am I? by giving students clues about the different house-building careers and having them name the careers. Example: *I use a wrench to put together the pipes in your house so you can take a bath. Who am I? (plumber)* You may wish to play a variation of this game by playing What Am I? to review the information students have learned about different tools. Example: *I am used to pound nails into lumber. What am I? (hammer)*

13. Have students count objects that they have studied in this section of the unit (page 24).

14. Help students make Big Books (pages 25-28), using a poem and pattern pages.

15. Work with students to create edible houses (page 29). Allow time for students to eat the houses they make.

16. Invite a variety of guest speakers (page 30) representing the different careers that students have studied in this section of the unit. Have students sign thank you notes for the guests (page 33).

17. Arrange for students to take a field trip to a construction site or a building supply store (page 31). Name tag patterns are included on page 33. Have students wear name tags while on the field trip.

18. Create file-folder games to review the key vocabulary and concepts (page 34).

8

Flannel Patterns

Use the patterns shown below and on page 10 to create flannel board pieces. Display the pieces as you sing "This Is the Way We Build a House" (page 7). You may wish to use the flannel board pieces as you read aloud *Building a House* by Byron Barton. You may also wish to have students help you display the appropriate pieces on the flannel board.

Machine Operator

Hammer and Saw

Cement Mixer

Bricklayer

Carpenter with Hammer

Carpenter with Wooden Beam

Flannel Patterns *(cont.)*

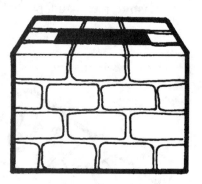

Chimney

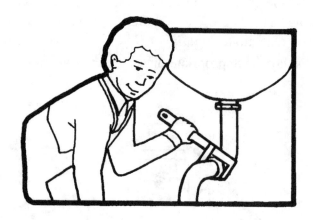

Plumber

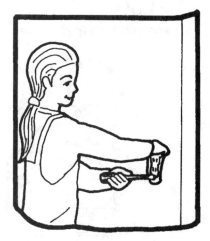

Electrician

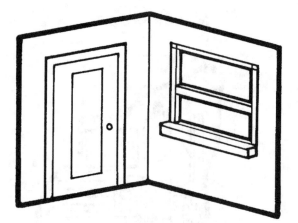

Door and Window

Painter

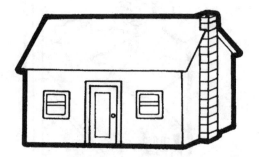

Completed House

Building a House Filmstrip

Use the directions shown below to have students make a filmstrip viewer. Make copies of the "filmstrips" on page 12. Ask students to color the filmstrip pictures. Then tape the strips together in the correct order to show how a house is built. Help students slide the filmstrip through the slits in the viewer.

Materials:

- Filmstrip viewer pattern (page 11)
- White posterboard
- Filmstrips (page 12)
- Crayons or markers
- Transparent tape

Directions for the filmstrip viewer:

Step 1: Cut out the following pattern.

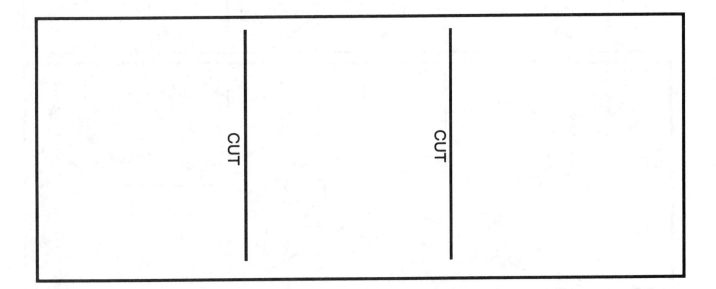

Step 2: Trace the pattern onto pieces of white posterboard.

Step 3: Cut slits as shown on the pattern.

Step 4: Allow students to color a landscape (trees, bushes, flowers, etc.) on the ends of the viewers.

Step 5: After students have completed their filmstrips, have them slide them into their viewers.

Building a House Filmstrip *(cont.)*

Directions:

Step 1: Cut out the strips that are shown below.

Step 2: Have students color the strips.

Step 3: Tape the strips together in the correct order.

Step 4: Show students how to use the viewers (page 11) to watch their filmstrips.

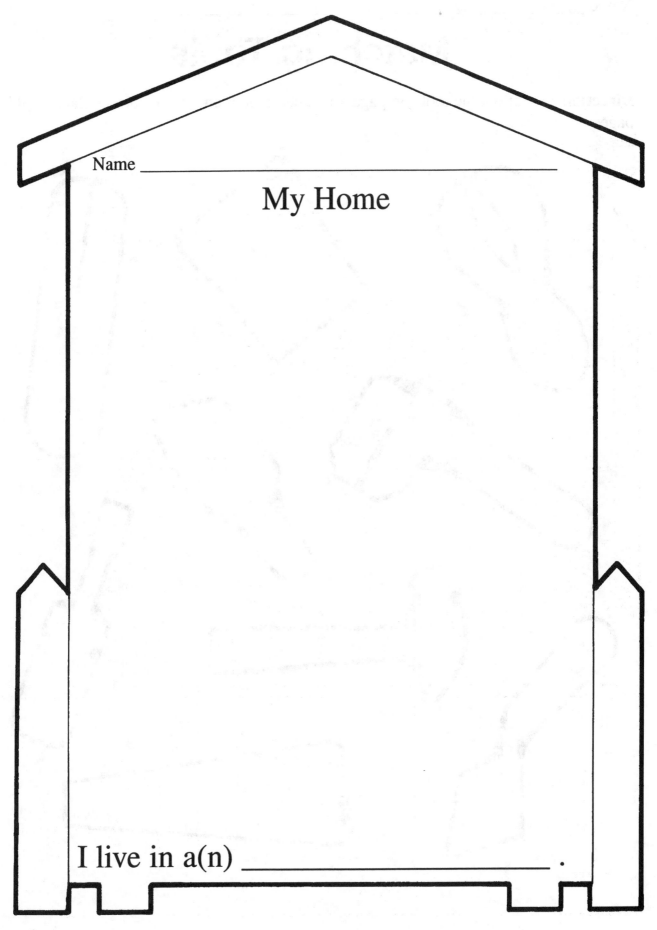

Name _____

My Home

I live in a(n) _____ .

Name _____

Matching Tools

Directions: Cut out the tools on page 15. Then glue them in the correct place on this page.

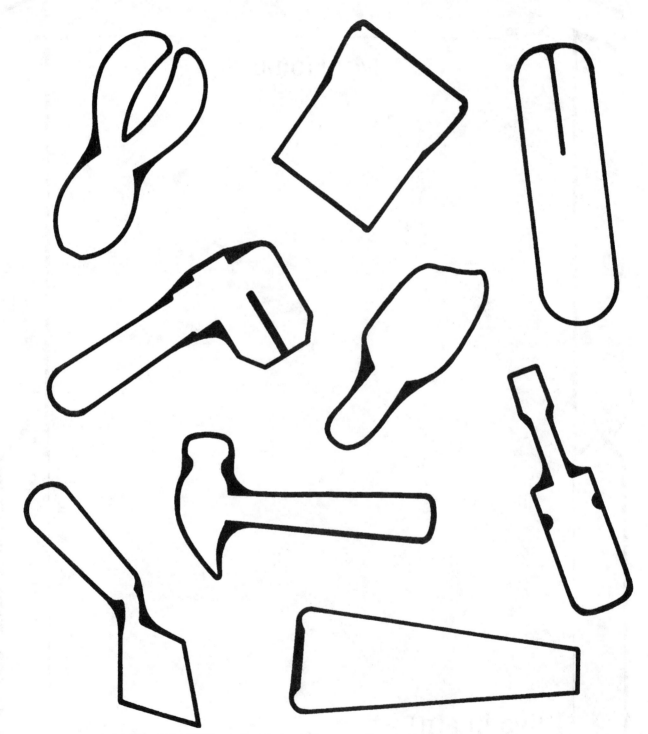

Matching Tools *(cont.)*

Directions: Cut out the tools on this page. Then glue them in the correct place on page 14.

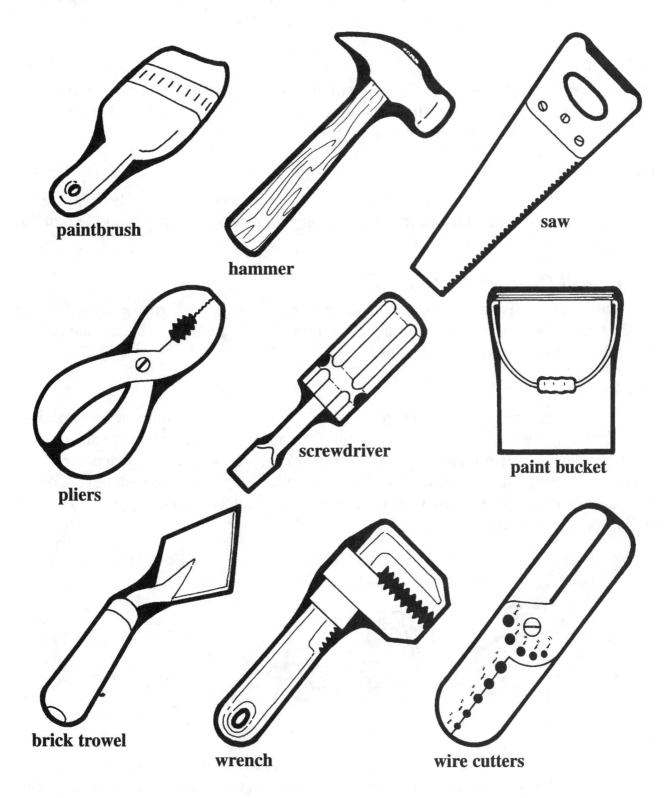

paintbrush

hammer

saw

pliers

screwdriver

paint bucket

brick trowel

wrench

wire cutters

I Want to Be an Equipment Operator

Storytime

Read aloud a story about equipment operators. See the bibliography (pages 79-80) for suggestions. Discuss the pictures and the text with students.

Role-Play

Have students role-play the jobs that an equipment operator does. You may wish to have students make simple props for their role-play. For example, they might sit in chairs or large boxes and pretend that they are driving their equipment.

Discussion

Ask students what they would like about being an equipment operator. Then ask them what they would dislike. Record the information on a chart. You may wish to point out that likes and dislikes are opposites.

Equipment Operator Center

Put sand or dirt in dish pans or in a sand table if one is available. Provide toy bulldozers for students to pretend they are equipment operators digging a hole to build a house. Additional centers are suggested on page 5.

Movement

Have students compare the different types of equipment that an equipment operator uses. Have students imitate the movement of each. For example, students can imitate a backhoe by holding their hands together to form a cup, stooping down, pretending to scoop up dirt, rotating on their feet to the left or right, and pretending to dump the dirt. Ask students to compare the movement they make for each type of equipment. Then ask the following questions:

1. How does a bulldozer move?

2. How does a backhoe move?

3. How does a dump truck move?

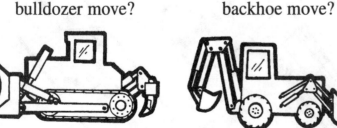

Manipulative

Follow the directions on page 17 to prepare copies of the Equipment Operator Puzzle. Encourage students to take home their puzzles. Place an extra copy of the puzzle in the Activity Center (page 5) for students to enjoy while studying this section of the unit.

Equipment Operator Puzzle

Directions: For each student, glue a copy of the puzzle onto a piece of poster board. Allow students to color their copies of the puzzle. Laminate the puzzles, or cover them with clear contact paper. Cut out the pieces and place each set in a reclosable plastic bag or an envelope for students to take home. Have students work with family members to put the puzzles together. Encourage students to tell their families what they have learned about the community workers who build our homes.

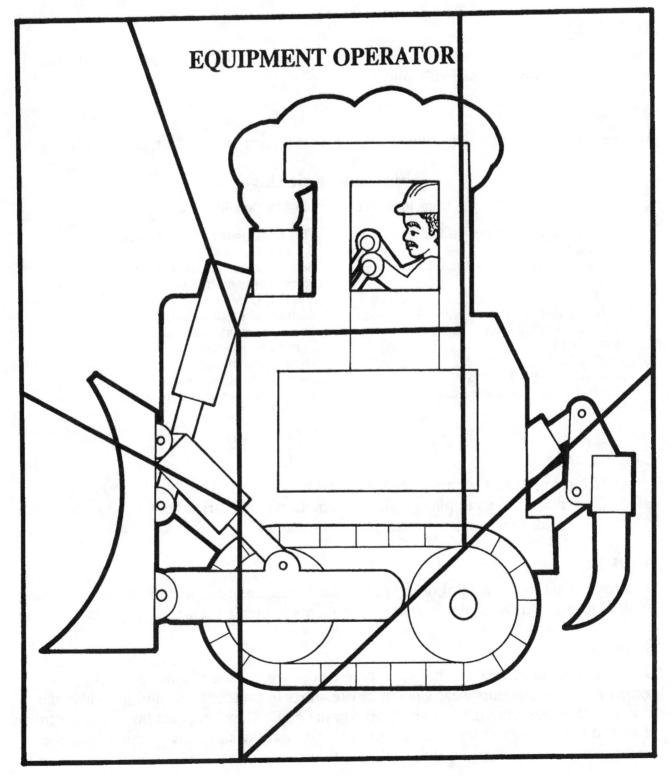

EQUIPMENT OPERATOR

I Want to Be a Bricklayer

Storytime

Read aloud a story about bricklayers. See the bibliography (pages 79-80) for suggestions. Discuss the pictures and the text with students. While reading the story, show the tools that a bricklayer uses.

Role-Play

Have students role-play the jobs that a bricklayer does. You may wish to have students make simple props for their role-play.

Music

Have students pantomime the movements of a bricklayer as they sing the following song.

This Good Bricklayer

(Sing to the tune of "Old MacDonald")

This bricklayer had some bricks,
E-I, E-I, O.
And with his (her) tools he (she) stacked some bricks.
E-I, E-I, O.
With a brick-brick here,
And a brick-brick there,
Here a brick!
There a brick!
Everywhere a brick-brick.
This bricklayer had some bricks,
E-I, E-I, O.

This bricklayer had some bricks,
E-I, E-I, O.
Between these bricks he (she) spread some mortar,
E-I, E-I, O.
With some mortar-mortar here,
And some mortar-mortar there,
Here some mortar!
There some mortar!
Everywhere some mortar– mortar
This bricklayer had some bricks,
E-I, E-I, O.

Block Center

Have students pretend they are bricklayers and build a wall from blocks found in the Block Center. Tell them to place white construction paper strips between the blocks for the mortar. Additional centers are suggested on page 5.

Art Ideas

Add some sand to fingerpaint or tempera paint to represent the texture of the mortar used by bricklayers. Allow students to use these paints to create pictures.

Science

Obtain some mortar mix and bricks. These can be purchased at a builders' supply company. Have students wear smocks or old shirts to protect their clothing. Mix the mortar with water according to directions on the bag. Show students how to use a trowel to spread the mortar as they stack the bricks. You may wish to have students use the bricks to create something useful, such as a flower box.

I Want to Be a Carpenter

Storytime and Role-Play

Read aloud a story about carpenters. See the bibliography (pages 79-80) for suggestions. Discuss the pictures and the text with students. While reading the story, show the tools that a carpenter uses. Have students role-play parts of the story using toy or imaginary tools.

Carpentry Center

Display pictures of things that carpenters make, such as houses, cabinets, and furniture. Provide play tools and wood samples for students to use. Additional centers are suggested on page 5.

Hard Hat Pattern

Have students make hard hats, using the following directions. Allow them to wear the hard hats during storytime, when working at a center, or during independent play.

Directions:

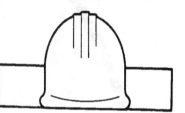

Step 1: Make copies of the hard hat pattern on page 20. Glue them onto construction paper.

Step 2: Have students color and cut out the hard hats.

Step 3: Cut 2-inch (5 cm) wide strips of tagboard for the bands.

Step 4: Staple each hard hat to a band. Adjust the band to fit the student's head and staple.

Poem

Have students imitate the actions described as they recite the following poem with you.

Pound Goes the Hammer (Author Unknown)

Pound pound pound pound pound
goes the hammer.
Pound pound pound pound pound pound pound.
Bzz bzz bzz bzz bzz
goes the big saw.
Bzz bzz bzz bzz bzz bzz bzz.
Chop chop chop chop chop
goes the big axe.
Chop chop chop chop chop chop chop.

Listening

Have students listen to songs about carpenters. See the bibliography (page 80) for suggestions. Then record sounds on a cassette tape of different tools being operated, and have students guess which tool is making the sound.

Hard Hat Pattern

See page 19 for directions.

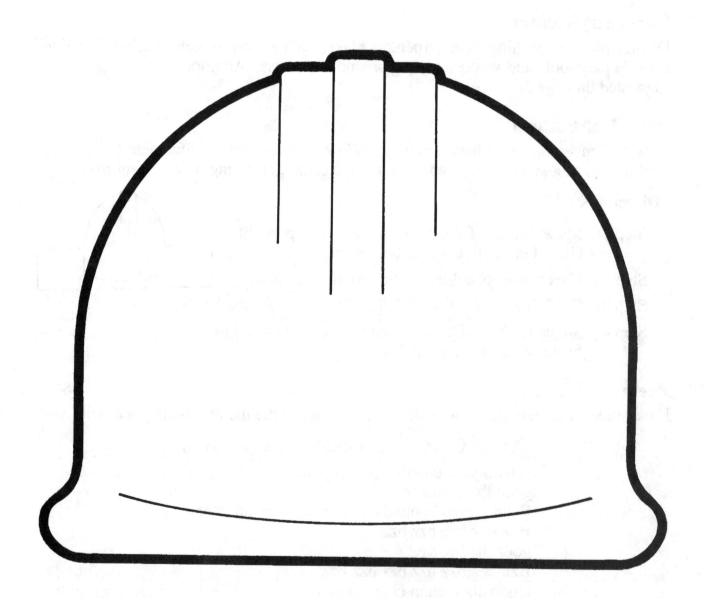

I Want to Be a Plumber

Storytime and Role-Play

Read aloud a story about plumbers. See the bibliography (pages 79-80) for suggestions. Discuss the pictures and the text with students. While reading the story, show the tools and a variety of pipes that a plumber uses. Have students role-play parts of the story using toy or imaginary tools and pipes.

Plumbing Center

Have pipes of various lengths and sizes, pipe wrenches, elbow joints, couplings, etc., for students to examine and use during independent playtime. Additional centers are suggested on page 5.

Art

Give students heavy pieces of posterboard and have them draw pictures of houses or make enlarged copies of the house pattern (page 32) for students to glue onto the posterboard. Tell students to pretend that they are plumbers and have them glue straws onto the posterboard to simulate pipes in a house.

Science Discussion

Explain to students how the water that comes into homes and the school is taken from ground water sources (lakes, rivers, reservoirs, etc.) and underground water sources (aquifers), cleaned at treatment plants, and sent through pipes so they can use it. Then tell students what happens to water after it is used. Ask students a variety of questions related to the discussion. Suggested questions: *Why do we need pipes in a house? What are pipes made from? Where does the water come from that goes through the pipes? Where does the water go after we use it?*

Math

Show students both metal and plastic pipes. Have them compare the sizes by asking the following questions: *Which pipe is the longest? Which pipe is the shortest?* Have them compare the weights by asking the following questions: *Which pipe is the heaviest? Which pipe is the lightest?* You may wish to have students use a balance scale to determine which pipes are heavier than others.

Health

Show students a pipe that is an elbow joint. Ask students to find places on their bodies that bend like the pipe. Lead students to conclude that they can bend their arms at the elbows and their legs at the knees like the pipe. Turn the pipe so that it bends in different directions. Have students use their arms to show how the pipe bends.

School Tour

Take a tour of your school, locating places where there are pipes. Ask students what they think it would be like in a school without indoor plumbing.

I Want to Be an Electrician

Storytime and Role-Play

Read aloud a story about electricians. See the bibliography (pages 79-80) for suggestions. Discuss the pictures and the text with students. While reading the story, show the tools and a variety of wires that an electrician uses. Have students role-play parts of the story, using toy or imaginary tools.

Discussion

Have students imagine what their lives would be like without electricity. Close the blinds and doors to the classroom. Then turn off the lights. Ask students to brainstorm a list of ways that you could light up the room without turning on the lights. Possible answers include *flashlights, opening the blinds, candles,* and *gas-powered lanterns.*

Electrician Center

Have different shapes, sizes, and colors of wire; flashlight bulbs in holders; and batteries for supervised experimentation with electricity. Additional centers are suggested on page 5.

Music

Have students listen to songs about electricians. See suggestions in the bibliography (page 80). You may wish to have them sing along or role-play being electricians during the songs.

Math

After students examine samples of electrical wires ask if the wires are the same color, size, or shape. Strip away the insulation from some of the wires. Show students that sometimes there is one wire inside and other times there are several wires. Have students count the number of wires inside the insulation.

Combining Music, Math, and Movement

Before having students sing the song shown below, write the numbers one through ten on pieces of construction paper. Give each student a number. Ask students to stand up whenever their numbers are mentioned in the song.

Ten Little Electricians
(Sing to the tune of "Ten Little Indians")

One little, two little, three electricians,
Four little, five little, six electricians,
Seven little, eight little, nine electricians,
Ten electricians wiring the house.

I Want to Be a Painter

Storytime and Role-Play

Read aloud stories about painters. See the bibliography (pages 79-80) for suggestions. Discuss the pictures and the text with students. You may wish to have students role-play parts of the stories.

Painter Center

Provide the following materials in the center: paint samples, pieces of wood, paper, various colors of paint, various sizes of paintbrushes, and painters' caps. Allow students to use these materials during independent playtime. Additional centers are suggested on page 5.

Art

Provide cups with different colored paints, including black and white. Supervise as you allow students to experiment by mixing paints to see what colors they can create. Allow students to use the paints to make pictures on large sheets of butcher paper.

Music and Movement

Have students sing and pantomime the actions with imaginary or real paintbrushes.

This Is the Way We Paint a House

(Sing to the tune of "Here We Go 'Round the Mulberry Bush")

This is the way we paint a house
Paint a house, paint a house.
This is the way we paint a house
When we go to work.

Up is the way we paint a house
Paint a house, paint a house.
Up is the way we paint a house
When we go to work.

Down is the way we paint a house
Paint a house, paint a house.
Down is the way we paint a house
When we go to work.

Right is the way we paint a house
Paint a house, paint a house.
Right is the way we paint a house
When we go to work.

Left is the way we paint a house
Paint a house, paint a house.
Left is the way we paint a house
When we go to work.

This is the way we paint a house
Paint a house, paint a house.
This is the way we paint a house
When we go to work.

Science

Tell students that rainbows have certain colors (red, orange, yellow, green, blue, indigo, violet), and they always appear in the same order. Point out that all of the colors may not always be visible. Have students use watercolors or tempera paints to create rainbows. After it rains, have students look for rainbows in the sky. Ask them to identify the colors that they see.

Name _____

Count the Objects

Directions: Count the objects. Write the correct number in each box.

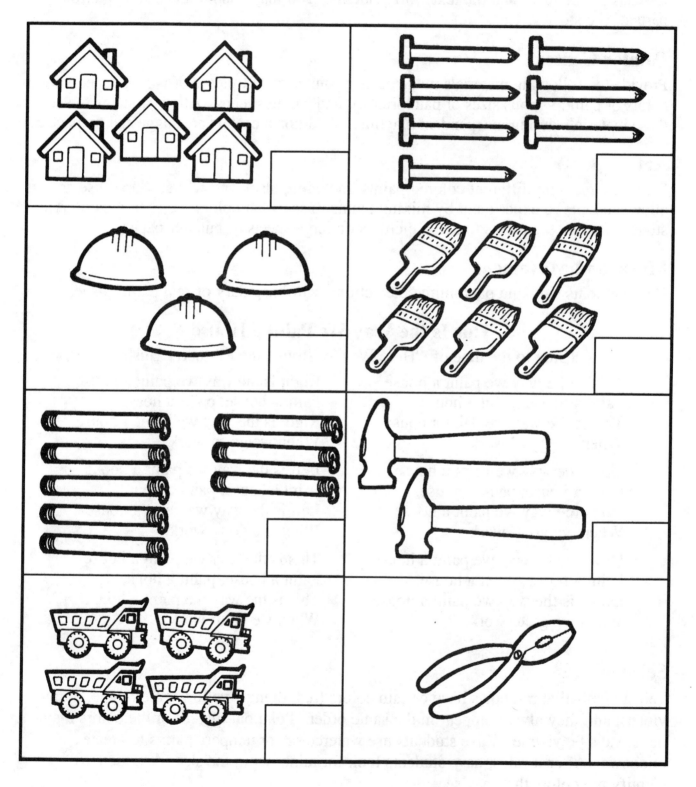

Let's Make Big Books

Have students create Big Books by enlarging the patterns on pages 25-28. Have them use crayons or markers to color their Big Books. Copy the following poem, one line on each page, or have students dictate language experience stories and write the stories in their Big Books. Have students draw pictures of their families on the last page of their books. Discuss the process of building a house as students construct their Big Books.

The House (Traditional)

This is the roof of the house so good.
These are the walls that are made of wood.
These are the windows that let in the light.
This is the door that shuts so tight.
This is the chimney so straight and tall.
What a good house for us, one and all.

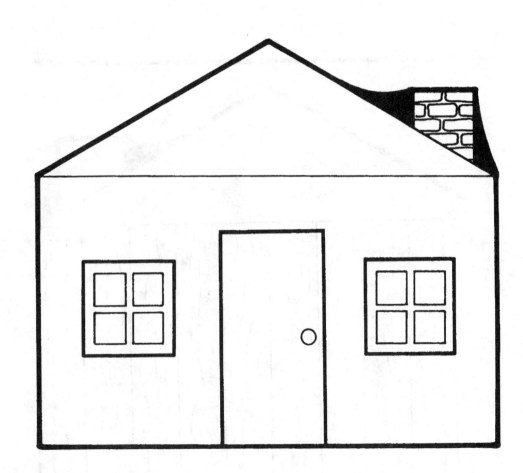

Let's Make Big Books *(cont.)*

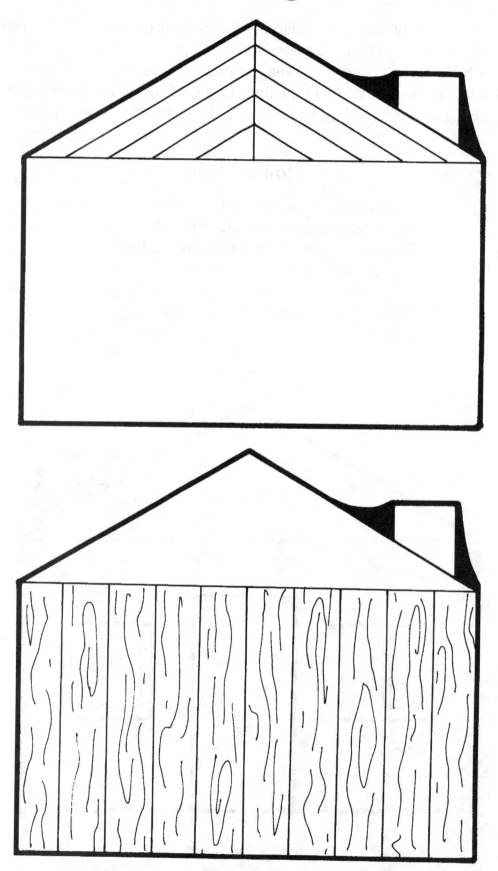

Let's Make Big Books *(cont.)*

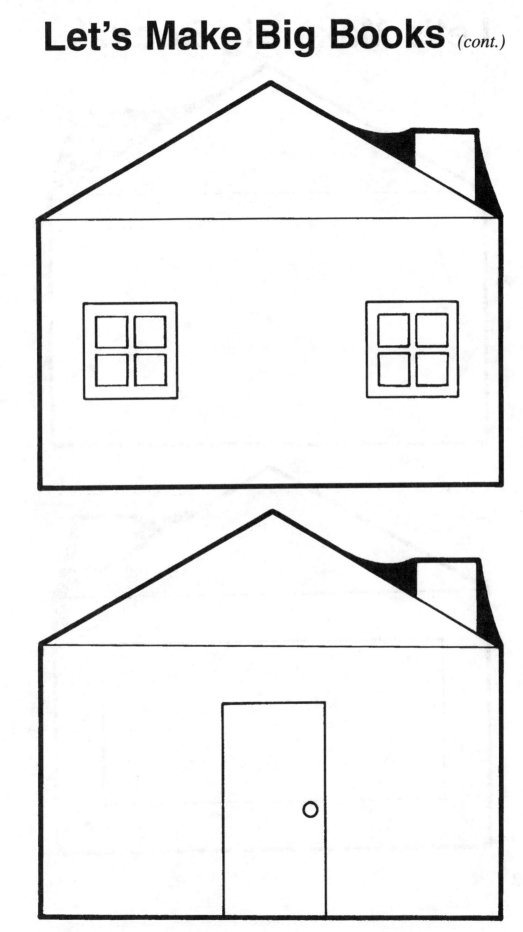

Let's Make Big Books *(cont.)*

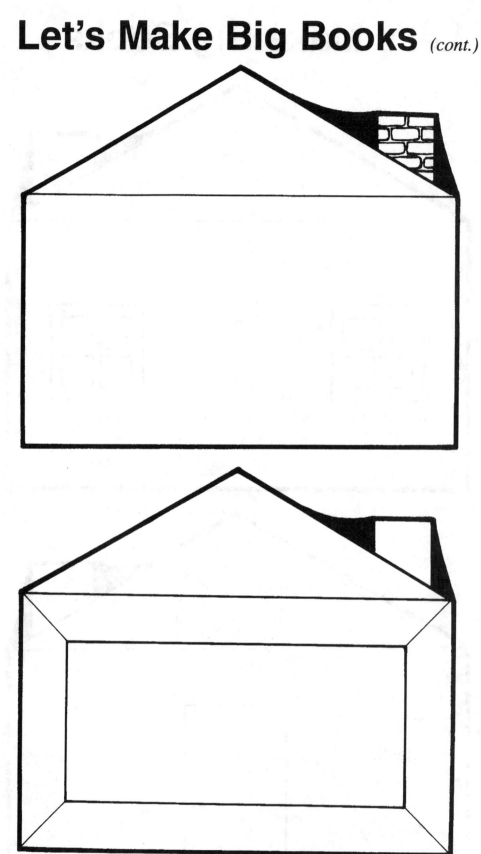

Edible Houses

You may wish to have parent volunteers or older students help your class make these edible houses. Before using these activities, be sure to check with parents to see whether students have any food allergies or dietary restrictions.

Option 1: A Bread House

Ingredients:

- Peanut butter
- Crackers
- Wheat bread
- White bread
- Pastry brushes
- Food coloring
- Milk
- Can of spray cheese
- Aluminum foil
- Knife

Directions:

Be sure to orally describe each step as you take students through these directions. Place a slice of wheat bread on a piece of aluminum foil. Use a knife to cut a rectangular piece of white bread for the house and a triangular piece for the roof. Then spread some peanut butter on half of a small cracker and place it on the wheat bread for the chimney. Spray some cheese above the cracker to make swirls of "smoke" coming from the chimney. Mix a few drops of food coloring into small cups of milk. Have students use pastry brushes to "paint" their houses. Use the knife to cut a second piece of wheat bread into a rectangle and two squares. These will be the door and the window. Spread a small amount of peanut butter on the rectangle and squares and stick them onto the piece of white bread in appropriate places. You may wish to toast the sandwiches before students eat them.

Option 2: A Gumdrop House

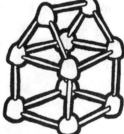

Ingredients:

- Gumdrops
- Toothpicks

Directions:

Place a gumdrop on each end of a toothpick. Continue to connect toothpicks and gumdrops to form a house as shown.

Option 3: A Gingerbread House

Ingredients:

- Gingerbread
- Gumdrops, raisins, icing, candy sprinkles, etc., for decorating

Directions:

Use your favorite gingerbread recipe to create a gingerbread house. Then have students help you decorate the house with a variety of ingredients.

Guest Speakers

Invite people from the community, such as equipment operators, carpenters, plumbers, bricklayers, electricians, and painters, to come and speak to students about how a house is built. Encourage the guests to tell about their personal experiences and show the tools they use to do their jobs. You may wish to help students prepare a list of questions they want to ask before the guest speakers come to visit. Use the thank you note on page 33 to send to the guest speakers.

Invitation

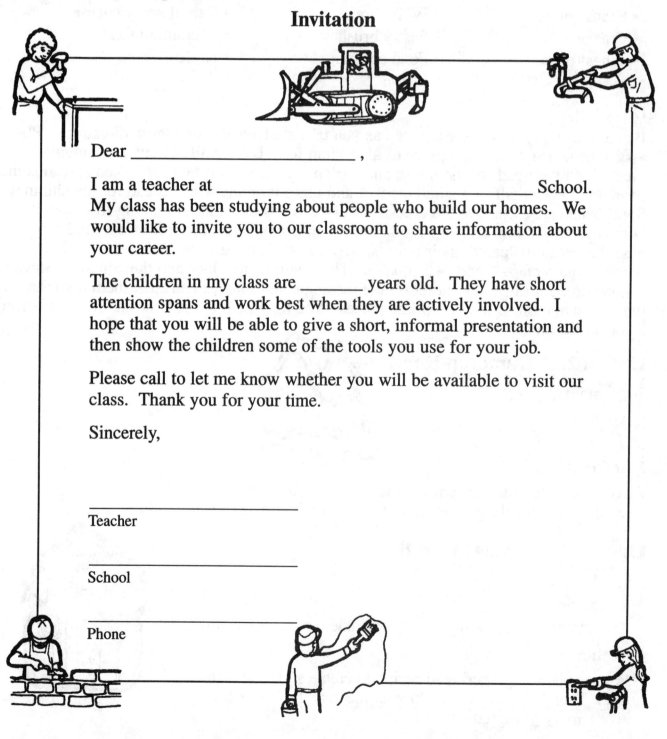

Dear _____ ,

I am a teacher at _____ School. My class has been studying about people who build our homes. We would like to invite you to our classroom to share information about your career.

The children in my class are _____ years old. They have short attention spans and work best when they are actively involved. I hope that you will be able to give a short, informal presentation and then show the children some of the tools you use for your job.

Please call to let me know whether you will be available to visit our class. Thank you for your time.

Sincerely,

_____
Teacher

_____
School

_____
Phone

Field Trips

Option 1: A Construction Site

Make arrangements for your class to visit a construction site where houses are being built. Be sure to discuss the importance of following safety rules before going on the field trip. Invite parents to join you. Videotape the trip if possible. After the trip, have students draw pictures of houses being built.

Option 2: A Builders' Supply Store

Take your class to a builders' supply store. Have students examine the materials and tools used for building houses. After returning to the classroom, make a chart with the headings *Materials* and *Tools*. Have students name items they saw at the store. Write the item names under the appropriate headings.

Option 3: A Walking Tour

Take a walk around your neighborhood. During the walk, have students observe and discuss the sizes, shapes, and colors of different houses. Have students describe how the houses are alike and how they are different. You may wish to record students' observations on a note pad for later discussion.

Field Trip Permission Slip

We are going to: _____ .

The date for the trip is: _____ .

We will leave school at: _____ and return at: _____ .

Other important information: _____

- -

Child's Name: _____

☐ My child has permission to go on the field trip.

Parent's Signature: _____

Bulletin Board

Use the following bulletin board idea to introduce this section of *Community Workers.* The patterns below make the bulletin board quick and easy to create. Begin by covering the background with blue butcher paper. This will be the sky. You may wish to use white butcher paper or cotton balls to make some clouds in the sky. Staple strips of green butcher paper or artificial grass along the bottom of the bulletin board to create the ground. Then use an opaque projector to enlarge and copy the patterns shown below. Make several copies of the house pattern. Glue photographs of your students in the windows of the houses. Make multiple copies of the tools and place them around the border. Finally, create the title, "Who Are the People Who Build Our Homes?"

Thank You and Name Tags

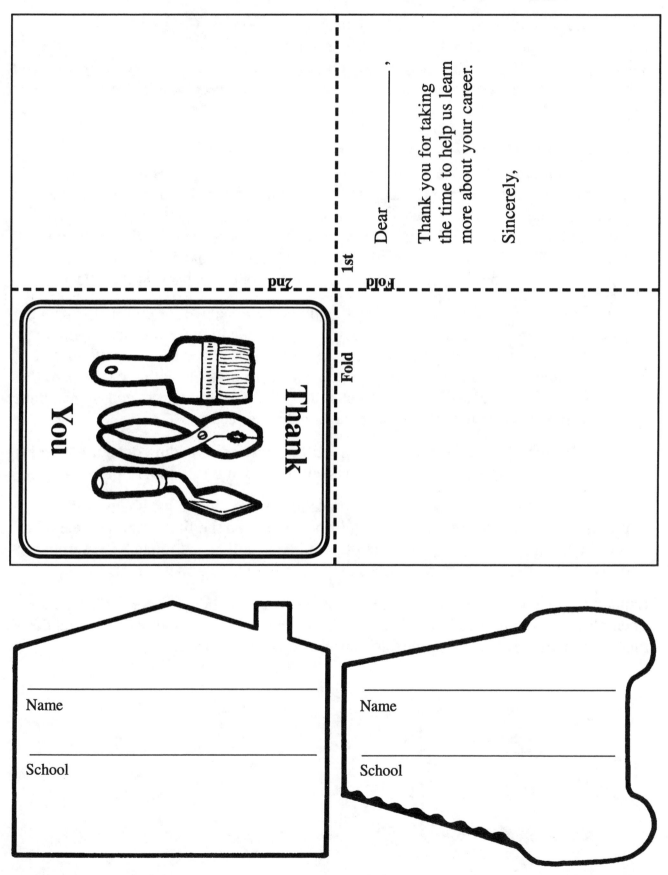

File-Folder Games

Materials: File folders, Markers, Wallpaper sample books*, Colored adhesive dots, Scissors, Crayons, Construction paper, Glue or rubber cement

*Note: Wallpaper sample books can be obtained from decorating and wallpaper stores. These are valuable resources for making file-folder activities, bulletin-board letters and backgrounds, as well as decorative displays.

Directions for Different Types of File-Folder Activities:

- **Color Matching:** Choose a pattern and trace it onto eight pieces of different colored construction paper, making two copies of the pattern on each color. Cut out the pattern pieces and glue one set onto the inside of a file folder. The other set will be used for matching. Add details to both sets with markers. For durability, laminate the completed file folder and the matching pieces. Place the matching pieces in a reclosable plastic bag. Then staple or glue the bag onto the back of the folder.

- **Dot Number Matching:** Follow the directions shown above for cutting the pattern pieces and storing the matching pieces. You may wish to make this activity more difficult by using only one color of construction paper. Place the same number of adhesive dots on each of two pieces. Glue one set of patterns with the dots onto the file folder. The other set is used for matching. The numeral that matches the number of dots may be written on the back of each matching piece.

- **Shape Matching:** Follow the above directions. Instead of adding dots, use markers to draw shapes (squares, circles, triangles, etc.) on each set of pattern pieces.

- **Pattern Matching:** Use wallpaper samples to cut two pieces, using any pattern pieces you wish. One set of patterns will be glued onto the file folder, and the other set of patterns will be used for matching. Students will have to match the wallpaper design for each set of patterns. Store the matching pieces as described above.

Explain to students how to use the file-folder activities and how to care for the pieces. Then place the file folders in the Activity Center (page 5). You may wish to send these file-folder activities home for students to use with family members.

The Best Teacher in the World

by Bernice Chardiet and Grace Maccarone

Summary

In this story, Ms. Darcy asks her student, Bunny, to take a note to another teacher, Mrs. Walker. Bunny is so excited about taking the note that she forgets to ask where Mrs. Walker's classroom is. Bunny is too embarrassed to go back and ask Ms. Darcy, so she wanders the halls, looking for the right room. She never finds Mrs. Walker's room. When Bunny returns to her own classroom, Ms. Darcy asks if she gave the note to Mrs. Walker. Bunny lies and says that she did. Bunny feels very guilty and stays home sick the next day. The following day Bunny tells Ms. Darcy what happened. Ms. Darcy tells Bunny that she should never be afraid to ask questions.

Suggested Activities

SETTING THE STAGE

1. Allow students to preview the book by reading aloud the title and showing them the pictures. Ask them what they think the book will be about.

2. Create different centers (page 5).

3. Display the bulletin board for People Who Help Us Learn (page 47). You may also wish to have a fellow teacher or parent volunteer take photographs of you while you are working with students. Then display the photographs as part of the border for the bulletin board.

4. Discuss the purpose of classroom rules. Then pick three or four rules and write them on poster board. Suggested rules: *Be polite to others. Keep your hands, feet, and objects to yourself. Use your quiet voice.* Be sure students understand the consequences for breaking the classroom rules. Review the rules and consequences on a daily basis.

5. Take students on a tour of your school building. Have them identify the different places in the building, such as the office, library, cafeteria, music room, art room, and gym. After returning to the classroom, you may wish to draw a simple map of your school building for students. Have students identify different places on the map and label them. Point out cardinal directions (north, south, east, west) as you work with the map.

6. Ask students to name the kind of people who work in your school building. When you take a tour of the building as suggested above, have students identify people by their specific job titles, such as teacher, counselor, secretary, principal, custodians, and cook. You may wish to invite some of the people who work in your building to visit your class and tell about their careers.

7. Have students listen to songs about teachers or school. See the bibliography (page 80) for suggestions.

8. Explain to students what rhyming words are. Then have students brainstorm a list of rhyming words for *book*. Suggested answers include *brook, cook, crook, hook, look, shook,* and *took.* Have students name rhymes for other words related to teachers and school, such as *learn, chalk,* and *teach.*

Suggested Activities *(cont.)*

ENJOYING THE BOOK

1. As you read the book, have students role-play different scenes. Discuss the pictures and the text. Be sure to talk about topics covered in the story, such as asking questions and lying.

2. Use the flannel board pieces (page 38) as you read the book or use the poems and songs on pages 39 and 42.

3. Discuss what kinds of things a teacher does. Then ask students whether they think they would like to be teachers. On the chalkboard, write the names of students who would like to be teachers. Have students count how many names are on the chalkboard. Then have them check to see whether more boys or more girls would like to be teachers.

4. Explain to students that a diorama shows a setting in miniature. Have students bring shoe boxes to class. Then ask them to work in cooperative learning groups to create dioramas of classrooms or schools. Display the dioramas in the library.

5. Have students complete the activities that focus on teachers and how they help us learn (page 39).

6. Explain to students what a maze is. Then have each of them draw a line to show the correct route through a maze, starting at a picture of a teacher and ending at a picture of the teacher's desk (page 40). You may wish to draw other mazes related to teachers and classrooms for students to use. The pictures shown at the beginning and end of the maze can be drawn or cut out from school supply catalogues and glued onto the paper with the maze.

7. Follow the directions to prepare copies of the Classroom Puzzle (page 41) for students. Show students how to put the puzzle together. Ask them to identify the different things they see in the completed puzzle. Have them compare and contrast the classroom shown on the puzzle with their own classroom. Place the puzzles in reclosable plastic bags or envelopes. Encourage students to take their puzzles home to share with their families.

8. Show students pictures, filmstrips, films, or videos of schools, classrooms, and teachers from around the world. Have them compare and contrast the different schools, classrooms, and teachers.

9. Have the class make a Big Book entitled *My Teacher.* Ask students to draw pictures of themselves working with a teacher to learn different kinds of skills. Then work with students to write a language experience story on the pages of the Big Book. Make a cover for the book, using posterboard. Punch holes on the left side of the cover and the pages. Bind the book together, using yarn or metal rings. To assemble the Big Book, see the illustrations on page 46. After the book has been assembled, read it to students. Place it in the Activity Center (page 5) so students can read it as often as they like.

10. Discuss how it feels to be embarrassed. Point out that everyone feels embarrassed at times. Ask volunteers to tell about times that they felt embarrassed. Have students brainstorm some solutions to avoid embarrassing situations.

11. Display photographs of people at your school who help children learn, such as teachers, librarians, assistants, etc. (page 47). Discuss the jobs that these people do.

Suggested Activities (cont.)

EXTENDING THE BOOK

1. Discuss with students the different people who help us learn. Point out that many people, such as parents, librarians, athletic coaches, and ministers, also help us learn. Ask students to name things that their parents have taught them. Suggested answers include: *tying shoes, riding bikes, being polite, walking,* and *talking.* Then use the following poem with students. After reading the poem, have students draw pictures of their parents helping them learn something.

My Parents

My Parents take good care of me.
They are so special, don't you see?
They teach me all that's fair and good,
So I can do the things I should.
They are so patient and so kind,
And better parents I couldn't find.
My parents mean the world to me.
They are so special, don't you see?

2. Tell about different types of jobs at a library, such as being a children's librarian, reference librarian, bookmobile librarian, and library clerk. Ask students whether they would like to be librarians.

3. Review with students how to write the numbers one through ten. Have students count pictures of library books and write the appropriate numbers in each box (page 43).

4. Make copies of the Book Size Matching Cards (page 44). Cut apart the cards and show students how to make matching pairs according to the sizes of the books. Allow students to mix and match their own set of cards. Then demonstrate how to play Concentration using the cards. Have each student work with a partner and play the game. To vary the activity, you can use the Book Size Matching Cards to reinforce color recognition. Divide the cards into pairs, regardless of the sizes of the books. Color each set of two books the same color. Have students make matching pairs based on the colors of the books.

5. Complete one or more of the culminating activities for this section of the unit (page 45).

6. Arrange for students to take a field trip to the public library (page 46). Have them wear name tags shaped like books (page 46).

7. Create file-folder games (page 48) to review the key vocabulary and concepts.

8. Have students use small paper bags to create puppets of teachers or librarians. To reinforce what students have learned about People Who Help Us Learn, invite them to have their puppets tell about their jobs as teachers or librarians. You may wish to have students take their puppets to another class and tell those students what they have learned about teachers and librarians.

9. Have students brainstorm a list of words that begin with each letter in the word *teacher.* For example, students might suggest the words *two, tape,* and *towel* for the letter *t.*

Flannel Patterns

Use the following patterns to create flannel board pieces. Display the pieces as you read aloud *The Best Teacher in the World,* by Bernice Chardiet and Grace Maccarone, or use the poems and songs on pages 39 and 42. You may wish to have students help you display the appropriate pieces on the flannel board.

Student

Teacher

Librarian

Student

I Want to Be a Teacher

Storytime and Role-Play

Read aloud some stories about teachers. See the bibliography (pages 79-80) for suggestions. Discuss the pictures and text with students. You may wish to have students role-play different parts of the stories. Invite students to vote for their favorite books about teachers. Show the results of the vote on a bar graph. Ask students questions about the bar graph. Suggested questions: *Which book was liked the most? Which one was liked the least?*

Teacher Center

Place teaching materials such as pens, pencils, chalk, small chalkboards, books, and papers in the center. Have students pretend that they are teachers using these materials. Additional centers are suggested on page 5.

Music

Invite students to listen to songs about teachers. See the bibliography (page 80) for suggestions. Have them sing along and imitate the actions described in the lyrics.

Poem

Have students brainstorm a list of things that teachers do to help them. Write the list on the chalkboard. Use the list to write a poem about teachers. Read the poem to students. You may wish to copy the poem onto a large chart tablet and use rebus symbols for some of the words so that students can help you read it. Have students role-play being the teacher in front of the class as you read the poem together.

Physical Education

Adapt the game of Simon Says by calling it Teacher Says. Have students follow your directions whenever you say *"Teacher says. . ."* before giving the directions. If you do not say *"Teacher says. . ."* before giving the directions, students should remain still. Examples: *Teacher says clap your hands.* (Students clap their hands.) *Hop on one foot.* (Students do not move.)

A Maze

Have students draw a line to show the correct route through the maze, starting at the picture of a teacher and ending at the picture of the teacher's desk (page 40).

Manipulative

Prepare copies of the Classroom Puzzle (page 41) for students. Allow time for students to put their puzzles together. If students have difficulty putting the puzzles together, you may wish to have them work with partners. Place a copy of the puzzle in the Activity Center (page 5) for students to use during independent playtime.

Name _____

Maze

Directions: Help the teacher find her desk. Draw a line from the teacher to her desk.

40

Classroom Puzzle

Directions: For each student, glue a copy of the puzzle onto a piece of poster board. Allow students to color their copies of the puzzles. Laminate the puzzles or cover them with clear contact paper. Cut out the pieces and place each set in a reclosable plastic bag or an envelope for students to take home. Have students work with family members to put the puzzles together. Encourage students to tell their families what they have learned about the community workers who help us learn.

A TEACHER HELPS US LEARN!

I Want to Be a Librarian

Storytime and Role-Play

Read aloud stories about libraries and librarians. See the bibliography (pages 79-80) for suggestions. Discuss pictures and text and have students role-play parts of the stories.

Music

Invite students to listen to songs about librarians. See the bibliography (page 80) for suggestions. Then sing the following songs together to the tune of "My Bonnie Lies Over the Ocean."

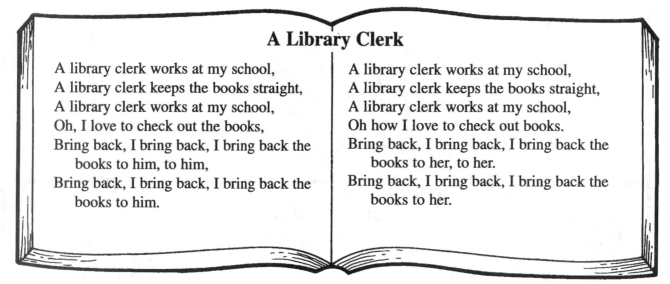

A Library Clerk

A library clerk works at my school,
A library clerk keeps the books straight,
A library clerk works at my school,
Oh, I love to check out the books,
Bring back, I bring back, I bring back the
    books to him, to him,
Bring back, I bring back, I bring back the
    books to him.

A library clerk works at my school,
A library clerk keeps the books straight,
A library clerk works at my school,
Oh how I love to check out books.
Bring back, I bring back, I bring back the
    books to her, to her.
Bring back, I bring back, I bring back the
    books to her.

Poem

Work with students to write about librarians, using a type of poem called a haiku. A haiku consists of three lines, with the first line having five syllables, the second having seven syllables, and the third having five syllables. Ask students to illustrate their haikus. Display the poems in the library.

Visiting the School Library

Arrange to take students to the school library. Ask your librarian to tell students about how a library is organized and how to use a card catalogue. Have the librarian tell about careers in a library, such as children's librarian, reference librarian, or library clerk.

Math

Have students count books and write the correct number in each box (page 43).

Manipulative

Have students use the Book Size Matching Cards (page 44). After students have learned how to match these cards at school, place them in envelopes and send them home for students to use with family members.

Name _____

Count the Library Books

Directions: Count the library books in each row. Then write the number in the box.

Name _____

Book Size Matching Cards

Directions: Cut out the cards and mix them up. Then match the cards with books that are the same size.

44

Celebration Day

Have students participate in a special celebration of the people who help us learn. Use the activities suggested below or create some of your own.

Skits and Puppet Shows: Have students present skits or puppet shows that are about people who help us learn.

Guest Speakers: Invite people from the community to come and speak to students about how they teach skills to other people. Guest speakers could include people who teach others how to play musical instruments, play sports, and create arts and crafts.

Murals: Have students draw murals that show how they learn from others.

Displays: Have students display the things they made during the activities in this section of the unit.

Book Drive: Have your class sponsor a book drive at your school. Give the book donations to your school or public library.

Science: Have students make recycled paper according to the directions shown below.

Materials:
- Newspapers
- Measuring cup
- Water
- Flat wooden board
- Blender
- Square pan
- Metal window screen

Directions:

Step 1:   Tear several pages of the newspaper into tiny pieces. Put the paper in a blender.

Step 2:   Add 5 cups (1250 mL) of water and blend until the paper has turned to pulp.

Step 3:   Pour about 1 inch (2.54 cm) of water into the square pan.

Step 4:   Cut a piece of window screen so it can fit into the square pan. Place the piece of screen in the pan.

Step 5:   Pour the pulp mixture over the screen, spreading it evenly.

Step 6:   Lift the screen and drain the water.

Step 7:   Open another section of the newspaper and place the screen with the mixture inside of it. Flip over the paper so the screen is on top.

Step 8:   Now place the flat wooden board on top of the newspaper which has the wire screen and mixture inside of it.

Step 9:   Press down hard on the board to squeeze out all of the excess water.

Step 10:   Remove the board, open the newspaper, and remove the wire screen.

Step 11:   Allow the mixture to dry for at least one day. After the mixture dries, carefully remove the paper. Allow students to use the paper to make a book or draw pictures.

Take a Field Trip

Arrange to take students on a field trip to the public library. Make copies of the name tag pattern shown below for the trip. While at the library, have the librarian give you a tour of the facilities. Point out how the public library and the school library are alike and how they are different. If possible take pictures of students while on the trip.

Name Tag Pattern

NAME   SCHOOL

Make a Field Trip Big Book

After returning to school, have students create a Big Book entitled *My Library Trip*.

Directions: Punch three holes on the left-hand side of six pieces of posterboard. Have students use one piece of posterboard to create a cover for their Big Book. Then have them use the rest of the posterboard to illustrate some of the things that they saw at the library. Ask students to dictate captions for the illustrations as you write them on the pieces of posterboard. Then help students hold the pieces of posterboard together and connect them with metal rings or yarn. Read aloud the Big Book to students. Then place the Big Book in the Activity Center (page 5) and allow students to enjoy reading it as often as they like.

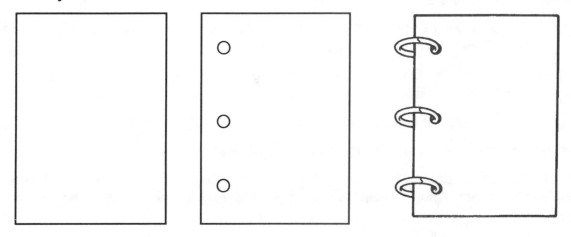

Bulletin Board

Use the following bulletin board idea to introduce this section of *Community Workers*. The patterns below make the bulletin board quick and easy to create. Begin by covering the background with butcher paper. Use an opaque projector to enlarge and copy the patterns shown below. Be sure the book pattern and crayons are made from butcher paper that is a color different from the background. Use white butcher paper to make the pages of the book pattern. Make multiple copies of the crayon pattern and place them around the border of the bulletin board. On the pages of the book pattern glue photographs of teachers, librarians, parent volunteers, and other people in your school who help students learn. Finally, create the title, "People Who Help Us Learn."

File-Folder Suggestions

Use the suggestions shown below or your own ideas for file-folder games related to People Who Help Us Learn. Follow the directions on page 34.

Match Computers with Capital and Lower Case Letters

Match Books with Numbers and Number Words

Police

by Ray Broekel

Summary

This book uses photographs and simple text to teach students about the police. It explains the things that rookies, or new police officers, have to learn at a police school. Information is presented about police uniforms, badges, and equipment. The book helps students realize that police officers do many jobs to help their community.

Suggested Activities

SETTING THE STAGE

1. As you read the book, have students role-play different scenes.

2. Create centers (page 5), and display the bulletin board (page 60).

3. Invite students to share what they know about the police and firefighters.

4. Ask students whether they watch television shows that have police officers or firefighters. Have them describe the kinds of jobs that these people do in the shows.

5. Have students make finger puppets, using the patterns shown below.

Suggested Activities *(cont.)*

ENJOYING THE BOOK

1. Show students pictures of police officers doing their jobs. Have them name pieces of equipment that the police use.

2. Use the flannel board pieces (page 52) as you read the book or use the poems and songs on pages 53 and 54.

3. Discuss how police officers and firefighters help people in your community.

4. Have students complete the activities to learn more about the police (page 53). Have them use the pattern to make handcuffs (page 53) that they can use when they role-play being police officers.

5. Show students pictures, filmstrips, or videos of what police officers look like from around the world. Have them compare and contrast how the police look in different places.

6. Have the class make Big Books about the jobs that police officers do. Ask them to draw illustrations for the book. Then work with students to write the text for the books. To assemble the Big Books, see the illustrations on page 46. After the books are assembled, read them to students. Then place the Big Books in the Activity Center (page 5) so students can enjoy them during independent playtime.

7. Arrange to take students on a field trip to a police station. Have an officer show students the equipment that the police use to do their jobs.

8. Discuss the similarities between rules and laws. Ask students why they think it is important to have rules and laws.

9. Invite a police officer to your class to speak to your students.

10. Discuss with students why police officers carry badges. Then copy the badge pattern shown below onto pieces of tagboard. Cut them out. Tape safety pins to the backs of the badges. Then pin the badges onto students.

Suggested Activities *(cont.)*

EXTENDING THE BOOK

1. Ask students whether they would like to work as police officers or firefighters. Make a list on the chalkboard of students' names who are interested in each career. Create a bar graph that shows how many students would like to be police officers and how many would like to be firefighters. Ask students to decide whether more or fewer students wanted to be police officers.

2. Remind students what rhyming words are. Have them name words that rhyme with *fire*. Possible answers include *buyer, crier, drier, hire, liar, tire,* and *wire*.

3. Trace the outlines of each student's body on a large sheet of butcher paper. You may wish to have parent volunteers or older students help you do the tracing. Have students color their body outlines to look like police officers or firefighters. Display the pictures along the classroom wall.

4. Provide toy police cars and fire engines for students to use during independent playtime.

5. Have students use the activities to learn about firefighters (page 54).

6. Follow the directions (page 55) to help students make fire chiefs' helmets (page 56).

7. Demonstrate an experiment for the class, showing how a fire can be extinguished (page 57).

8. Follow the directions to prepare copies of the Fire Engine and Police Car Puzzle (page 58) for students. Show students how to put the puzzle together. Place the puzzles in reclosable plastic bags or envelopes. Encourage students to take their puzzles home to share with their families. Place a copy of the puzzle in the Activity Center (page 5) for students to use at school.

9. Take students to a fire station. Have them examine a Fire engine and a fire truck. Ask students to compare and contrast the two vehicles. After returning to the classroom, have students tell what they would like and dislike about being firefighters.

10. Have students make the Wheel Pattern (page 59). Ask them to tell you what they have learned about police officers, police cars, firefighters, and fire engines as they turn the wheel.

11. Create file-folder games to review key vocabulary and concepts (page 61).

12. Provide pieces of white construction paper for students. Have them make collages that show how the police and firefighters help the community.

13. Discuss with students what they should do if they ever get lost. Tell them that they can ask a police officer or a firefighter for help.

14. Invite a firefighter to speak to your class. Have the firefighter put on his or her equipment so students will not be afraid if they ever need to be rescued from a burning building. Ask the firefighter to share personal experiences about all of the things he or she does on the job.

15. Take a walk around your school building. Have students look for things related to fire safety, such as fire extinguishers and fire alarms. Discuss fire safety procedures. Have students practice having fire drills; learn how to stop, drop, and roll; pretend to crawl out of a smoke-filled room; role-play calling 911.

16. Ask students what they think their community would be like if they did not have police officers and firefighters. You may wish to have students illustrate some of their ideas.

Flannel Patterns

Use the following patterns to create flannel board pieces. Display the pieces as you read aloud *Police* by Ray Broekel, or use them with the poems and songs on pages 53 and 54. You may wish to have students help you display the appropriate pieces on the flannel board.

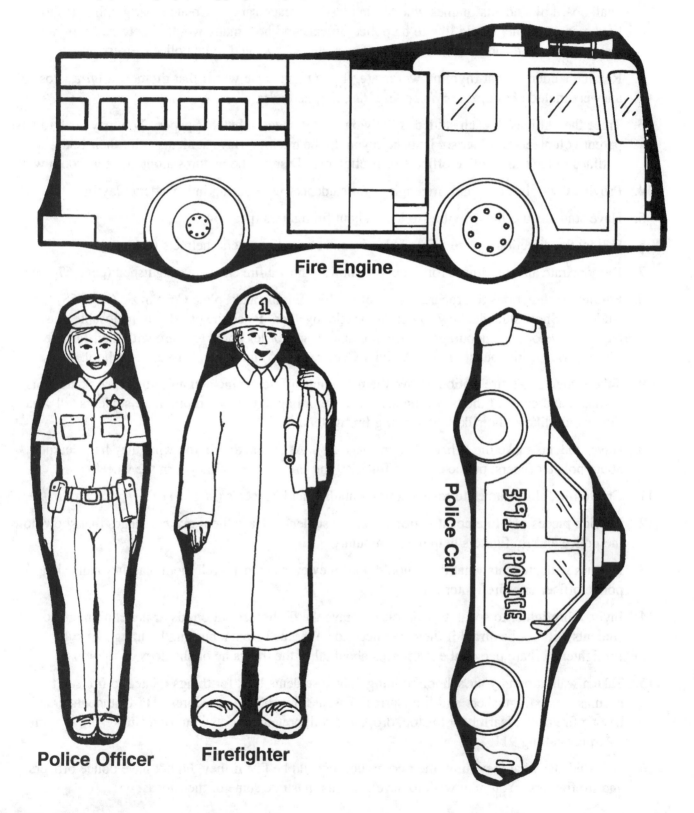

Fire Engine

Police Officer   **Firefighter**

Police Car

I Want to Be a Police Officer

Storytime and Role-Play

Read aloud stories about police officers. See the bibliography (pages 79 and 80) for suggestions. Discuss the pictures and text with students. You may wish to have students role-play parts of the stories.

Police Station

Save small milk cartons after they are emptied. Rinse them out with water and use glue or a stapler to reclose the tops. Have students use tempera paint to make the milk cartons look like police stations. See the illustration shown here.

Poem

Use the following poem with students. Ask them to pretend to be police officers and do the actions described in the poem.

Policeman
(Author Unknown)

There is a car driving down the street.
Here's the policeman walking his (her) beat.
Now he (she) is checking the stores at night,
To see that doors are locked up tight.

And this is a friendly traffic cop,
Who tells you when to go or stop.
When cars get in a traffic jam,
He (She) helps them better than anyone can.

Music

Play songs about police officers. See the bibliography (page 80) for suggestions.

Handcuffs

Enlarge the pattern shown below onto pieces of posterboard. Have students use posterboard, brads, and yarn to make sets of handcuffs. Students can use the handcuffs as they role-play being police officers.

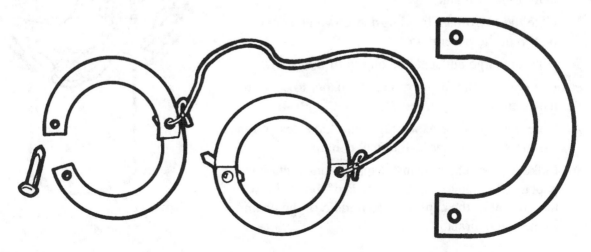

I Want to Be a Firefighter

Storytime

Read aloud stories about firefighters. See the bibliography (pages 79 and 80) for suggestions. Discuss the pictures and text with students.

Poem

Write the poem shown below on a large chart tablet. Have students do the actions described as you read the poem together.

Ten Brave Firemen (Author Unknown)

Ten brave firemen,
Sleeping in a row,
Ding goes the bell,
Down the pole they go.
Off on the engine,
Oh, oh, oh.

This is the fire engine,
This is the hose,
The firemen work very fast,
When the siren blows.
Up goes the ladder,
Out goes the hose,
The fire is out,
And that's the way it goes!

Fire Hydrant

Help students make a fire hydrant, using the directions and illustration shown below.

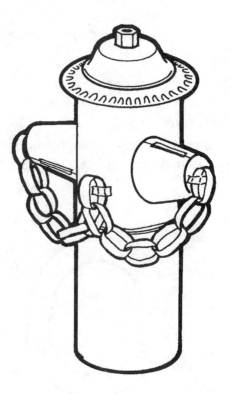

Materials: 2 cylindrical containers, construction paper, contact paper, paper plate, Styrofoam soup bowl, large nut, 2 paper cups, scissors, glue and tape, pencil

Directions:

Step 1: Use the construction paper or contact paper to cover the cylindrical containers.

Step 2: Glue the cylindrical containers together, end to end.

Step 3: Glue a paper plate upside-down onto the top cylindrical container.

Step 4: Glue the Styrofoam bowl upside-down and centered on top of the paper plate.

Step 5: Glue the large nut centered on top of the bowl.

Step 6: Use construction paper or contact paper to cover the paper cups.

Step 7: Glue the top of the paper cups onto the sides and in the middle of the top cylindrical container.

Step 8: Make a paper chain, using strips of construction paper. Use tape to attach the ends of the chain to the bottom of the cups and the middle of the chain to the fire hydrant.

Directions for a Fire Chief's Helmet

Materials:
- Red and yellow construction paper
- Tagboard or other sturdy paper
- Scissors
- Glue
- Markers

Directions:

Step 1: Reproduce the badge shown at the bottom of this page onto yellow construction paper or make a tagboard pattern for students to trace onto the yellow paper. Have each student cut out a badge and write a number on it.

Step 2: Reproduce page 56 onto tagboard to make a pattern for the helmet. Use scissors to cut on the interior solid line. Be sure you do not cut the dotted line; it is a fold line.

Step 3: Fold a piece of 12 x 18-inch (30 x 45 cm) red construction paper in half, widthwise.

Step 4: Place the flat end of the pattern against the fold. Trace around its outside edge, lift the flap, and trace around the interior section.

Step 5: While the paper is still folded, cut around the outside. Open and cut on the solid lines of the flap.

Step 6: Fold along the dotted lines.

Step 7: Glue the badge onto the flap of the helmet. Allow the glue to dry.

Step 8: Adjust the size of the hole to fit each individual's head. You may wish to add ties to each side of the helmet.

Badge Pattern

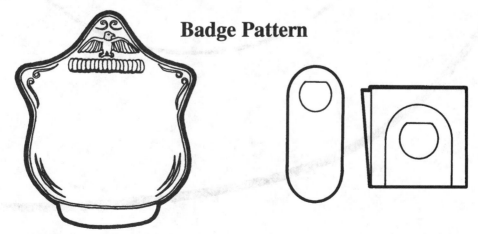

Pattern for a Fire Chief's Helmet

See page 55 for directions.

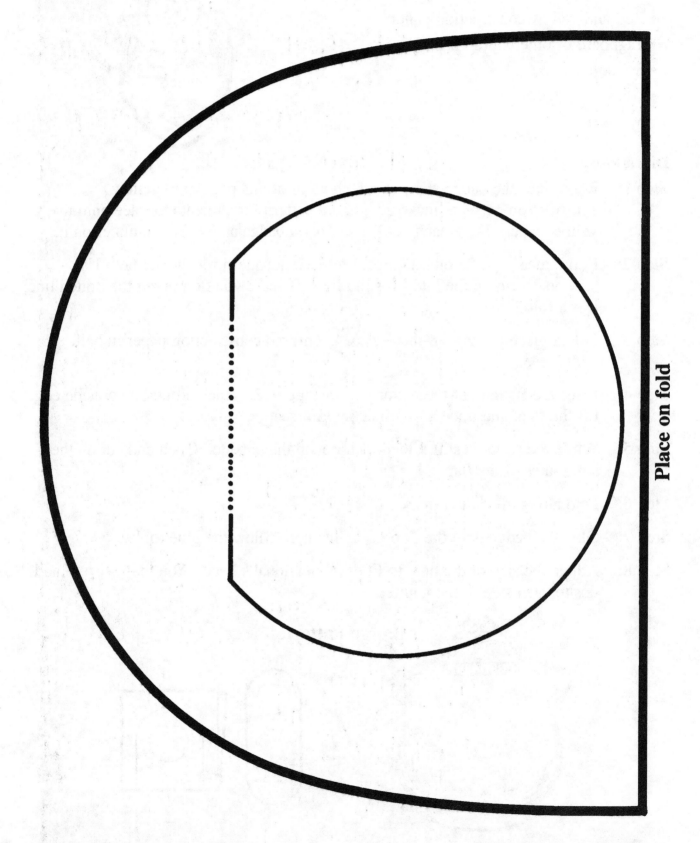

Place on fold

Extinguishing a Fire

Use the directions shown below to show how to fight a fire. Before doing this experiment, check to be sure that burning a candle is not against your school's fire safety code.

Materials:

- Small glass dish
- Candle
- Modeling clay
- Matches or lighter
- Spoon
- Vinegar
- Sodium bicarbonate

Directions:

Step 1: Place a small amount of modeling clay inside the glass dish at the bottom. Press the bottom of the candle into the clay. Be sure the top of the candle is lower than the top of the dish. If it is not, cut off the bottom of the candle.

Step 2: Use the spoon to put some sodium bicarbonate in the bottom of the dish around the candle.

Step 3: Carefully light the candle, using a match or lighter.

Step 4: Use the spoon to pour some vinegar over the sodium bicarbonate. Do not allow the froth to touch the flame of the candle. Ask students to describe what they observe.

(First, the vinegar makes the sodium bicarbonate froth. Then the candle goes out.)

Step 5: Explain that the vinegar mixes with the sodium bicarbonate to make a gas called carbon dioxide. Tell students that the carbon dioxide replaces the oxygen that the candle must have in order to burn.

Fire Engine and Police Car Puzzle

Directions: For each student, glue a copy of the puzzle onto a piece of posterboard. Allow students to color their copies of the puzzle. Laminate the puzzles or cover them with clear contact paper. Cut out the pieces and place each set in a reclosable plastic bag or an envelope for students to take home. Have students work with family members to put the puzzles together. Encourage students to tell their families what they have learned about the community workers who keep us safe.

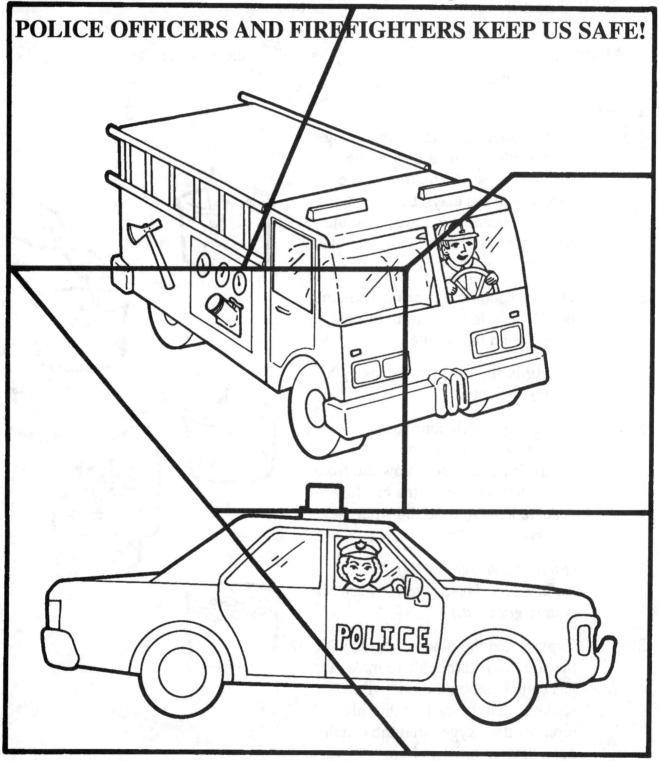

POLICE OFFICERS AND FIREFIGHTERS KEEP US SAFE!

Wheel Pattern

Directions:

Step 1: Cut out the pieces of the wheel.

police officer   police car

fire engine   firefighter

Step 2: Color the pictures. Hold the pieces of the wheel together as shown below. Stick a brad through the black dot in the middle.

Bulletin Board

Use the following bulletin board idea to introduce this section of *Community Workers*. The patterns below make the bulletin board quick and easy to create. Begin by covering the background with aluminum foil or white butcher paper. Then use an opaque projector to enlarge and copy the patterns shown below. Display newspaper articles about work done by your local police and fire departments under the appropriate vehicle. Ask students to draw pictures of police officers and firefighters in action. Use these pictures as the border of the bulletin board. Finally, create the title, "People Who Keep Us Safe."

File-Folder Suggestions

Use the suggestions shown below or your own ideas for file-folder games related to People Who Keep Us Safe. Follow the directions on page 34.

Match Fire Engine Sizes

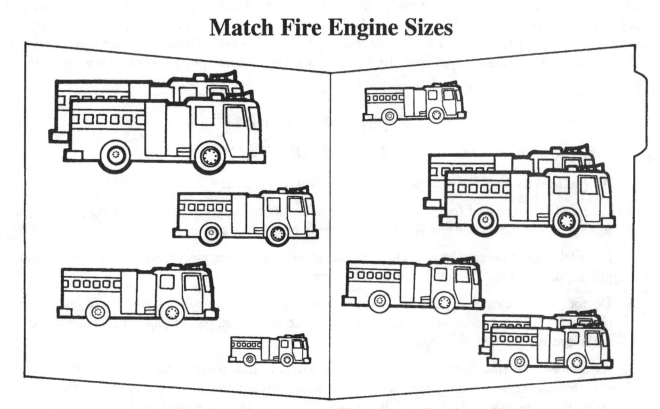

Match Numbers and Dots on Police Cars

Rita Goes to the Hospital

by Martine Davison

Summary

This informative book, developed by the American Medical Association, uses colorful illustrations and simple text to help young students understand why they might need to go to the hospital. The story is about a girl named Rita who gets her tonsils taken out at the hospital. Before the operation she meets the nurse, doctor, anesthesiologist, and nurse's aide. Rita feels more comfortable about being in the hospital after she meets all of the people who are there to help her stay healthy.

Suggested Activities

SETTING THE STAGE

1. As you read the book, have students role-play different scenes.

2. Create different centers (page 5). Collect the following materials to use as teaching props during this section of the unit. Then place these items in centers for students to use.

   Hospital Center: surgical gowns, caps, masks, gloves, bandages, x-rays, white shirts or hospital gowns, pads of paper, pencils, a small cot or mat.

   Doctor's Office Center: toy doctor and nurse medical kits, cotton balls, plastic bandages, gauze pads, roll of gauze, white shirts, pen light, eye chart, telephone, pad of paper, pencils, bathroom scale, growth chart, stethoscopes.

3. Ask students whether they have ever gone to a hospital. Discuss their feelings about those experiences. Have students name some of the reasons why someone might need to go to a hospital. Tell students the location of the closest hospital in your community.

4. Display photographs or pictures of the various people who work in hospitals, clinics, and doctors' offices. Discuss the types of jobs these people do.

5. Provide small mirrors for students to use. Ask them to look down their throats using the mirrors. Point out their tonsils to them.

6. Ask a parent volunteer who is involved in the medical field to come and show "real" medical equipment and let students hear each other's heart beat, etc.

7. Discuss how parents are people who help us stay healthy. Read the following poem with students. Have them role-play the poem.

My Mother (My Father)

My Mother (Father) knows the signs	She tucks me into bed,
That say I am sick.	And says that she can tell.
She hurries in to nurse me,	When I stop having fun,
She is so very quick.	Then I'm not feeling well.

Suggested Activities *(cont.)*

ENJOYING THE BOOK

1. Enlarge the medical career chart shown below onto posterboard or a large chart tablet. Have students choose medical careers that interest them. Discuss each student's medical career choice. Use the information from the chart to make a bar graph. Ask students questions about the information shown in the graph.

Medical Careers	Students' Names
Doctor	
Nurse	
Anesthesiologist	
Nurse's Aide	
X-ray Technician	
Optometrist	
Physical Therapist	
School Nurse	
Dentist	

2. Have students make hospital gowns like the one that Rita wore, using yellow butcher paper. Point out that yellow was Rita's favorite color. Ask students to name other things that are yellow. Then have each student tell what his/her favorite color is.

3. Use questions to stimulate a discussion about the story. Suggested questions: *Why did Rita need to go to the hospital? What people did Rita meet at the hospital? What food did Rita eat after her operation? How long did Rita stay in the hospital? Where did Rita's mom take her after they left the hospital? How do you think Rita felt about her stay at the hospital?*

4. Discuss with students why Rita had to eat ice cream after having her tonsils out. Ask students to name their favorite flavors of ice cream. Use the information to make a pictograph such as the one shown below.

5. Provide a variety of items that students might see at a doctor's office, such as plastic bandages, cotton balls, cotton swabs, rubber gloves, and tongue depressors. First have students count the objects. You may wish to have students write the number of objects on the chalkboard. Then show students how to use a balance scale. Allow them to experiment with balance scales to see which items weigh more than others. After students have had the opportunity to experiment with the scales, have them predict the answers to questions that you ask. Suggested questions include: *How many cotton balls will be equal in weight to one tongue depressor? Which will weigh more, a cotton swab or a cotton ball? Which will weigh less, four plastic bandages or four rubber gloves?* After students make their predictions, ask them to use the balance scales to determine whether they were right.

Suggested Activities *(cont.)*

EXTENDING THE BOOK

1. Contact your local hospital for donations of surgical scrub suits, discarded x-rays, and first-aid kits for students to take home at the end of this unit.

2. Arrange to take your class to a local hospital. After returning to the classroom, have a discussion about the things that students saw on the trip and how hospitals play an important role in maintaining people's good health. Talk about the different jobs that people working at a hospital do.

3. Read the following story to students. Have students paint a picture of Rita at the hospital.

Rita's Trip to the Hospital

In the hospital there are doctors and nurses
  who help Rita get well again.
The nurses take her temperature, blood
  pressure, and pulse.
They write the findings on Rita's chart.
The doctor comes to see Rita.
He listens to her heart
  and tells her about the operation.

Rita meets the anesthesiologist
  who will help her go to sleep.
They practice breathing together.
Although she is a little scared,
Rita feels much better now
They have all been so kind to her.
When it's all over, she gets to eat ice cream.
Hooray!

4. At circle time, talk with students about what makes them feel better when they are sick. Let students share their ideas about what they do when they feel sick and what their parents do to make them feel better. Explain that they will all have a chance to look for pictures of what makes them feel better and glue these pictures into a book they can look at again and again.

5. Have students learn about the ways in which doctors help keep people healthy (page 66).

6. Show students how to listen to the beats of their hearts using a homemade stethoscope (page 67).

7. Discuss the different types of jobs that nurses do (page 68), and invite your school nurse to talk to your class.

8. Focus on what a dentist does (page 69).

9. Have students role-play being dentists, using dental tools (page 69) and sets of teeth (page 70) that they make.

10. Have students complete the activities to learn what an optometrist is (page 71).

11. Follow the directions to prepare copies of the Eyeglasses Puzzle (page 72) for students. Remind students how to put the puzzle together. Place the puzzles in reclosable plastic bags or envelopes. Encourage students to take their puzzles home to share with their families.

12. Teach students what anesthesiologists, physical therapists, and x-ray technicians do (page 73).

13. Complete one or more of the Culminating Activities (pages 74–75) for this section of the unit.

14. Create file-folder games to review the key vocabulary and concepts (page 77).

    64

Flannel Patterns

Use the following patterns to create flannel board pieces. Display the pieces as you read aloud *Rita Goes to the Hospital* by Martine Davison or use the poems, stories and songs on pages 66, 68, 69, 71, and 73. You may wish to have students help you display the appropriate pieces on the flannel board.

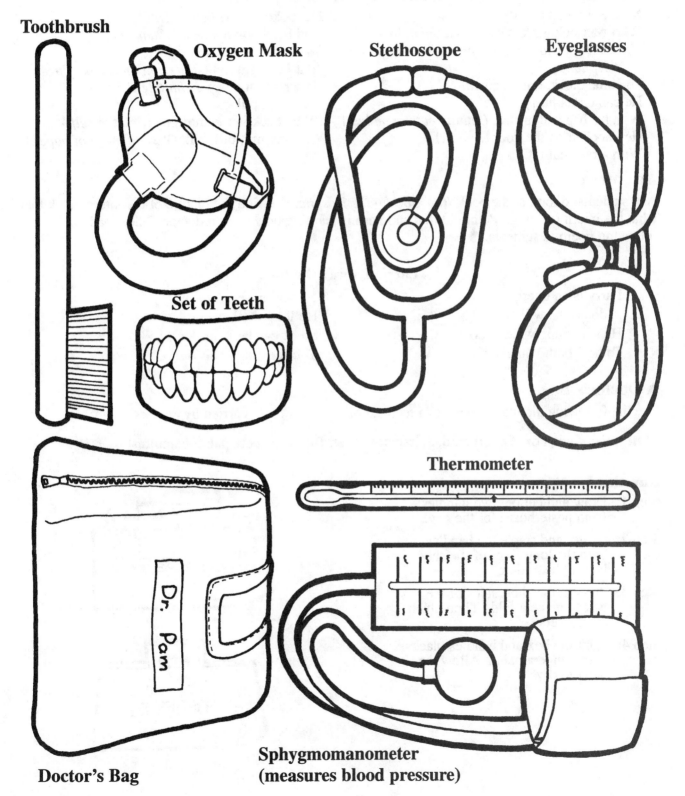

Toothbrush

Oxygen Mask

Stethoscope

Eyeglasses

Set of Teeth

Thermometer

Dr. Pam

Doctor's Bag

Sphygmomanometer
(measures blood pressure)

I Want to Be a Doctor

Fingerplay

Read aloud and act out the following fingerplay using appropriate props.

Miss Polly (Author Unknown)

Miss Polly had a dolly
Who was sick, sick, sick. *(Rock the baby.)*
She called for the doctor *(Imitate calling on the telephone.)*
To come quick, quick, quick.
He came in a hurry
With his bag and his hat. *(Imitate putting on hat.)*
He knocked on the door *(Knock.)*
With a rat-a-tat-tat.

He looked at the baby *(Cradle arms.)*
And he shook his head. *(Shake head.)*
So he said to Miss Polly
"Put her right to bed." *(Point and shake finger.)*
He wrote on a paper *(Imitate writing.)*
For a pill, pill, pill.
I'll be back in the morning *(Point to self.)*
With my bill, bill, bill. *(Wave a piece of paper.)*

An Intern

Ask students to look at the book *Rita Goes to the Hospital* and find the picture of the intern. Ask them what the intern is doing. Point out that an intern is learning how to be a doctor. Then read the following poem to students.

Larry (Laura), the Intern

Larry is an intern,
A doctor he will be.
He's learning what to do
To heal both you and me.

He will have to study,
He'll hardly have rest.
So he can be your doctor,
You see, that is his quest.

A Doctor's Bag

Use the following directions to make a medical bag such as those carried by doctors.

Materials: Shoe box, Posterboard, Scissors, Stapler, Black tempera paint, Paintbrush

Directions:

Step 1: Draw and cut out two handles from posterboard for the bag.

Step 2: Center and staple the handles onto the long sides of the shoe box in the middle.

Step 3: Press in the short sides of the box to make a fold. Then pinch the corners.

Step 4: Paint the box and handles black with tempera paint. Allow the paint to dry.

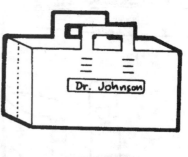

Make a Stethoscope

Materials:

- Plastic hose
- Funnel

Directions:

Step 1: Connect the plastic hose to the funnel.

Step 2: Carefully place the other end of the plastic hose near your ear.

Step 3: Place the funnel on a friend's chest.

Step 4: Listen to your friend's heart beat.

Step 5: Place the funnel on your chest, and listen to your own heart beat.

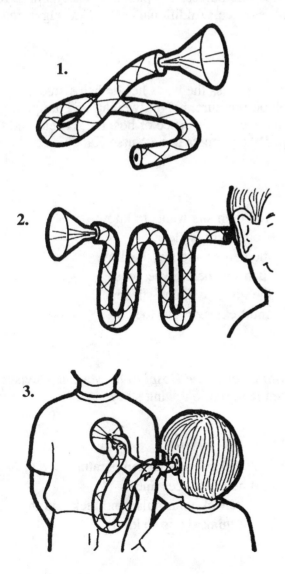

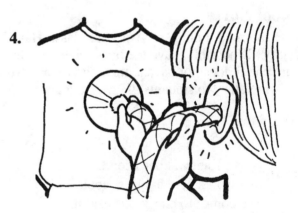

I Want to Be a Nurse

Storytime and Role-Play

Read aloud stories about nurses. See the bibliography (pages 79–80) for suggestions. Discuss the pictures and the text with students. Ask them to role-play different parts of the stories.

Discussion

Discuss the different types of duties nurses perform. Explain that nurses work in doctors' offices, health clinics, schools, and hospitals. Talk about the duties Nurse Abigail performed in the book *Rita Goes to the Hospital* by Martine Davison.

Music

Have students sing along with songs about nurses. See the bibliography (page 80) for suggestions.

Doctor's Office Center

Provide equipment that would be found in a doctor's office, such as bandages, medical bags, and stethoscopes (page 67). Have students pretend to be doctors, nurses, and patients. Ask them to role-play different scenarios about patients visiting a doctor's office. Additional centers are suggested on page 5.

School Nurse

Invite the school nurse to visit your class. Have her/him discuss the ways he/she helps students stay healthy. If possible, have the nurse check students' blood pressure, height, weight, and temperature. If your school does not have a nurse, invite one from a local doctor's office or hospital. Then read the following story to students. Have students create paper bag puppets to be Nurse Kaney.

Nurse Kaney

Nurse Kaney is our friend.
She works here at our school.
She comes to check our health.
She is so very cool.
She checks our ears and eyes,
To see if we can hear,

And then she wants to know
If our sight is clear.
She helps us to stay healthy,
Then just before she goes,
She gives us funny stickers,
And tickles on our toes.

Nurse's Aide

Have students find the picture of the nurse's aide in *Rita Goes to the Hospital* by Martine Davison. Discuss some of the jobs that a nurse's aide does. Then read the following story.

Mary (Larry), the Nurse's Aide

Mary is a nurse's aide,
The hospital is her place.
She'll get you water and a book,
And flowers in a vase.

She will check your temperature
And help you feel fine.
She'll check your pulse and tuck you in,
You'll think she is so kind!

I Want to Be a Dentist

Storytime and Role-Play

Read aloud stories about dentists. Discuss the text and pictures with students. Have them role-play different parts of the story.

Music

Have students listen to songs about dentists. For suggestions see page 80.

Discussion

Discuss what happens when you visit the dentist. See how many of the students in your classroom have been to a dentist. Discuss their experiences.

Classroom Visitor

Make arrangements to have a local dentist visit your classroom. Ask the dentist to show students the tools that he/she uses. If possible let him/her do dental screenings.

Poem

Read this poem to students. Ask them to illustrate the poem.

Dr. Sally, My Dentist

Meet my dentist, Dr. Sally,
She takes good care of me.
She tells me how to floss and brush,
She is so neat, you see.

And so my teeth are good and strong,
They'll last me all my days.
I eat the food that gives me health,
In, Oh, so many ways.

Dental Tools

Copy the patterns below to make dental tools that students can use as they role-play being dentists. Use a circle of aluminum foil for the mirror.

Make a Set of Teeth

Materials: Pencil, Cardboard, Pink tempera paint, Glue, Small macaroni, Masking tape, Scissors, Toothbrush

Directions:

Step 1: Use an opaque projector to enlarge and trace the pattern shown below onto pieces of cardboard. Make two copies of the pattern for each student.

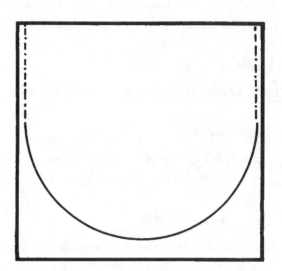

Step 2: Cut out the pattern pieces from the cardboard.

Step 3: Give students two of the cardboard pieces. Have them cover the pieces with pink paint. Allow the paint to dry.

Step 4: Help students place drops of glue along the curved edge of one piece of cardboard.

Step 5: Have students start by placing the open end of two pieces of macaroni in the middle of the curve on the cardboard. These will be the front teeth.

Step 6: Have students place the open end of pieces of macaroni along the curve.

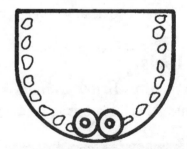

Step 7: Have students repeat steps 4-6 with the other piece of cardboard.

Step 8: Allow the glue to dry. Then place the pieces of cardboard together so the macaroni teeth are stacked on top of each other. Use two strips of masking tape to connect the pieces of cardboard along the flat edge.

Step 9: Have students pretend to be dentists and gently use toothbrushes to clean the sets of teeth.

I Want to Be an Optometrist

Storytime

Read aloud stories about optometrists. See the bibliography (pages 79 and 80) for suggestions. Discuss the pictures and the text.

Music

Have students listen to songs about optometrists. See the bibliography (page 80).

Poem

Read this poem to students. Have them do the actions described in the poem.

The Optometrist

An optometrist checks my eyes,
To see if I need glasses,
And if I need a pair,
They'll help in all my classes.

He helps me to see better,
To see both far and near,
And if I see him often,
I'll see my best all year.

My eyes are awfully precious,
I like to see the sky,
The clouds that roll across it,
The birds that fly so high.

I get my eyes checked often,
It is the thing to do,
To keep my eyes so healthy,
And you should do it too.

Eyeglasses

Trace the pattern shown below onto pieces of tagboard. Assemble the glasses and allow students to wear them during independent playtime or when role-playing.

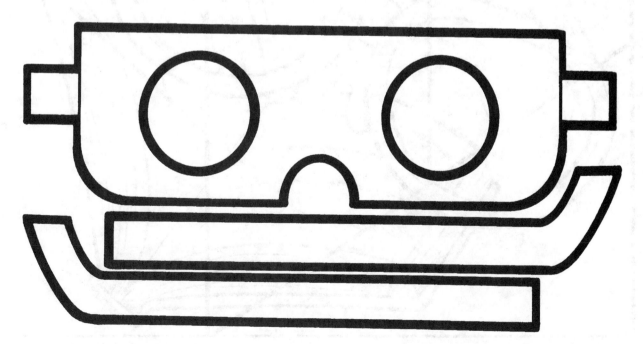

Eyeglasses Puzzle

Directions: For each student, glue a copy of the puzzle onto a piece of posterboard. Allow students to color their copies of the puzzle. Laminate the puzzles or cover them with clear contact paper. Cut out the pieces and place each set in a reclosable plastic bag or an envelope for students to take home. Have students work with family members to put the puzzles together. Encourage students to tell their families what they have learned about the community workers who help us stay healthy.

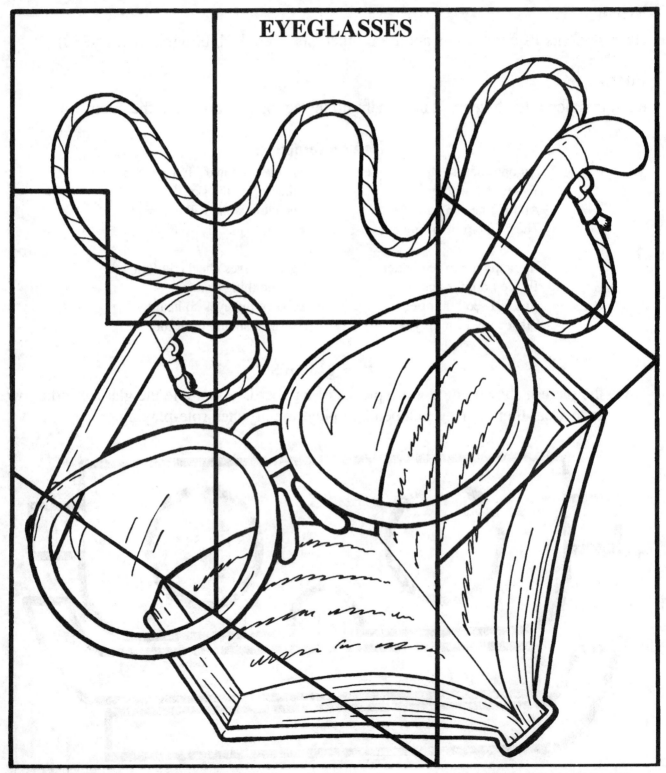

EYEGLASSES

I Want to Be an Anesthesiologist, Physical Therapist, or X-ray Technician

Anesthesiologist

- Discuss with students what job an anesthesiologist does.

- See how many of the students can say "anesthesiologist." Have students examine the pages in *Rita Goes to the Hospital* that show an anesthesiologist.

- Have them practice blowing up balloons to see whether they have strong lungs. Let students draw faces on the balloons, and then hang the balloons from the ceiling.

- Copy the following poem onto a large chart tablet. Read it to students.

Pat the Anesthesiologist

Oh, I am in a bed,
That moves both up and down.
My anesthesiologist
Has never worn a frown.

My anesthesiologist,
By the name of Pat,

Told me he would soothe me,
By my bed he sat.

The hospital is friendly,
My tonsils they will take,
Pat will stay beside me,
And help me when I wake.

Physical Therapist

- Discuss with students what a physical therapist does.

- Invite a physical therapist to speak to your class. Ask the therapist to show students what he or she does on the job.

- Read this poem to students.

The Physical Therapists

Helpers are physical therapists,
Who care for us when we ache.
They practice their healing arts,
Whenever a bone should break.

They stretch us and smooth us and guide us,
With crutches, a splint or a cane.
They are so very useful
In helping us ease our pain.

X-Ray Technician

- If possible, show students some X-rays and discuss what an X-ray technician does.

- Read this poem to students.

The X-ray Technician

X-ray technicians are ladies or men,
Who like to look beneath our skin.
With special film and cameras too,
They like to peek at what's within.

They can help the doctors know
What's going on when we are ill,
Or when we hurt or break a bone,
When we are sick or take a spill.

Healthfest

Art Activities

Cotton Swab Painting: Mix water and food coloring in a small bowl. Make several different colors. Encourage students to dip cotton swabs into a bowl and paint a picture. Have them use a different cotton swab for each color.

Cotton Ball Painting: Clip clothespins onto several cotton balls, one for each color of paint. Have students dip the cotton balls into the paint and create a picture.

Collage: Provide students with various materials, such as colored cotton balls, cotton swabs, tongue depressors, and plastic bandages. Encourage students to be creative as they make their collages with these materials.

Surgeon's Mask and Gown

To make a mask, use thick paper towels and fold them into thirds lengthwise. Punch holes into the middle of both ends. Attach yarn and tie. To make a gown, use butcher paper leaving it open in the back. Use a strip of material or a belt to tie the gown.

Manipulatives

Sorting Activity: Cover three one-pound coffee cans or margarine containers with construction paper. Attach a cotton swab to one can, a cotton ball to the second can, and a tongue depressor to the third can. Provide additional swabs, cotton balls, and tongue depressors for students to sort and place into the matching containers.

Alternate suggestions: This could also be done as a game. Divide students in two small groups and have them line up into two rows behind the starting line. Give each student in line an object. When the teacher says "Go!" students go to the cans and drop their objects into the correct one, then they go back of the starting line. The student who is next in line does the same thing. The first row of students who correctly get all of their objects into the cans wins the game.

Cotton Ball Bingo:

Cut out the cards and spinner from tagboard. Cut several cards with the colored circles in different places. Cover with clear contact paper. This game may be used with colored circles or with only the color words, depending on the students' developmental levels.

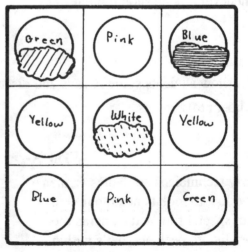

Big Book Pattern

Have students create Big Books by enlarging the pattern shown below. Have them use crayons or markers to color their Big Books. Ask students to dictate language experience stories about people who help us stay healthy.

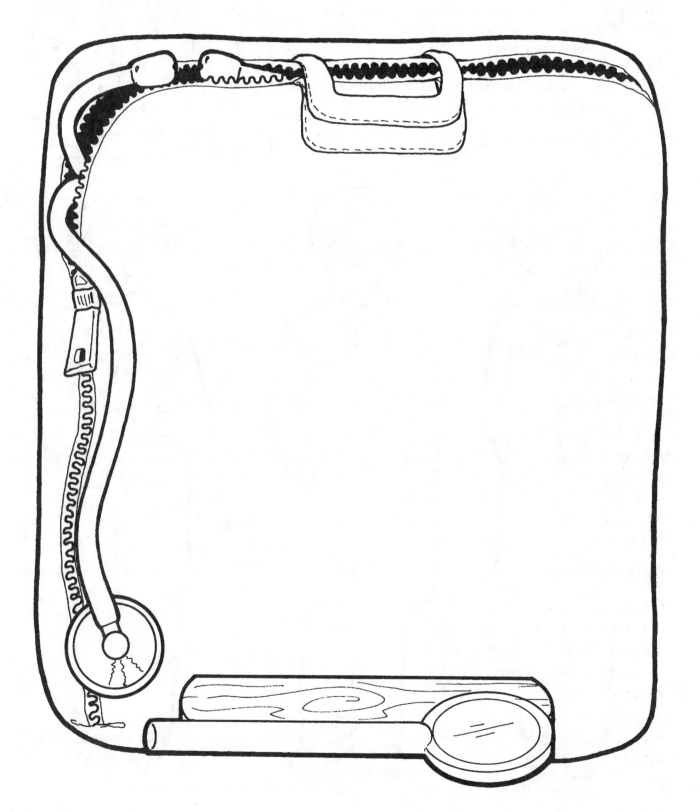

Bulletin Board

Use the following bulletin board idea to introduce this section of *Community Workers*. The patterns below make the bulletin board quick and easy to create. Begin by covering the background with white butcher paper. Then use an opaque projector to enlarge and copy the patterns shown below onto the white paper. Have students draw pictures of themselves at the doctor's office. Use these pictures as the border of the bulletin board. Finally, create the title, "People Who Help Us Stay Healthy."

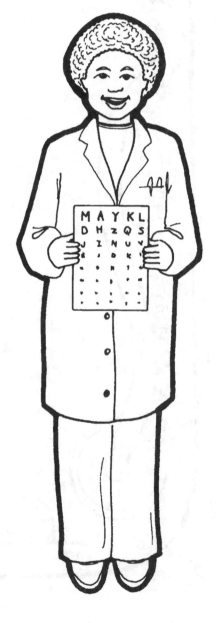

File-Folder Suggestions

Use the suggestions shown below or your own ideas for file-folder games related to
People Who Help Us Stay Healthy. Follow the directions on page 34 to create the file-
folder games.

Match Colors and Color Words on Plastic Bandages

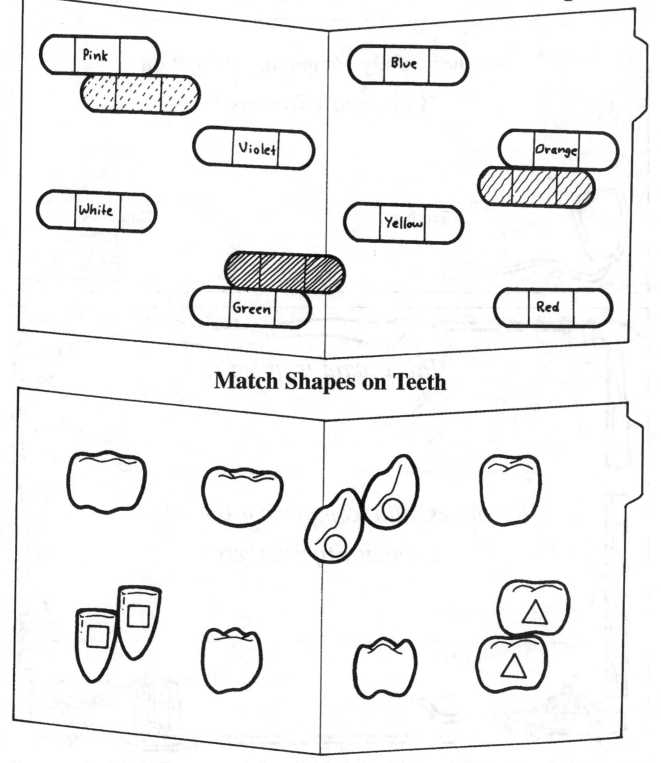

Match Shapes on Teeth

Community Workers' Awards

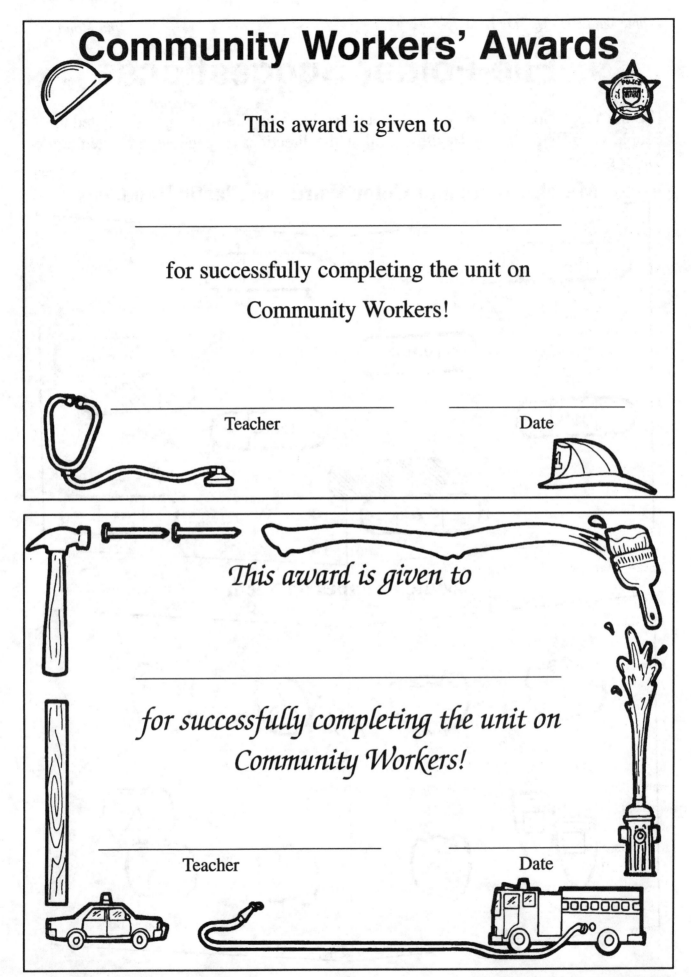

This award is given to

_____

for successfully completing the unit on

Community Workers!

_____   _____
Teacher   Date

This award is given to

_____

for successfully completing the unit on

Community Workers!

_____   _____
Teacher   Date

Bibliography

People Who Build Our Homes

Daniel, Kira. *Home Builder.* Troll, 1989.

Florian, Douglas. *A Carpenter.* Greenwillow, 1991.

Gibbons, Gail. *How a House Is Built.* Holiday, 1990.

Jennings, Terry. *Cranes, Dump Trucks, Bulldozers, and Other Building Machines.* Kingfisher, 1993.

Lillegard, Dee. *I Can Be a Carpenter.* Childrens, 1986.

Lillegard, Dee. *I Can Be a Plumber.* Childrens, 1987.

Lillegard, Dee and Wayne Stoker. *I Can Be an Electrician.* Childrens, 1986.

Morris, Ann. *Tools.* Lothrop, 1992.

Muntean, Michaela. *Wet Paint.* Western, 1990.

Pluckrose, Henry. *Build It!* Watts, 1990.

Robbins, Ken. *Tools.* Four Winds Press, 1983.

Royston, Angela and Graham Thompson. *Monster Building Machines.* Barron, 1990.

Shone, Venice. *Tools.* Scholastic, 1991.

Wood, Leslie. *My House.* Oxford University Press, 1988.

People Who Help Us Learn

Allard, Harry. *Miss Nelson Is Back.* Houghton, 1982.

Beckman, Beatrice. *I Can Be a Teacher.* Childrens, 1985.

Gibbons, Gail. *Check It Out! The Book About Libraries.* Harcourt Brace Jovanovich, 1985.

Giff, Patricia Reilly. *Next Year I'll Be Special.* Doubleday, 1993.

Greene, Carol. *I Can Be a Librarian.* Childrens, 1988.

Kimmel, Eric A. *I Took My Frog to the Library.* Viking, 1990.

Radlauer, Ruth Shaw. *Molly at the Library.* Simon & Schuster, 1988.

Yorke, Malcolm. *Richie F. Dweebly Thunders On!* Dorling, 1994.

People Who Keep Us Safe

Barrett, Norman S. *Picture World of Fire Engines.* Watts, 1990.

Barrett, Norman S. *Picture World of Police Vehicles.* Watts, 1990.

Bond, Felicia. *Poinsettia and the Firefighters.* Crowell, 1984.

Brown, Margaret Wise. *The Little Fireman.* HarperCollins, 1993.

Elliot, Dan. *A Visit to the Sesame Street Firehouse.* Random House, 1983.

Fowler, Richard. *Mr. Little's Noisy Fire Engine.* Putnam, 1990.

Hankin, Rebecca. *I Can Be a Firefighter.* Childrens, 1985.

Hannum, Dotti. *A Visit to a Police Station.* Childrens, 1985.

Hutchings, Amy and Richard. *Firehouse Dog.* Scholastic, 1993.

Johnson, Jean. *Police Officers: A to Z.* Walker, 1986.

Marston, Hope Irvin. *To the Rescue.* Cobblehill, 1991.

Matthias, Catherine. *I Can Be a Police Officer.* Childrens, 1984.

Munsch, Robert. *The Fire Station.* Annick Press, 1991.

Nau, Patrick. *State Patrol.* Carolrhoda, 1984.

Pellowski, Michael J. *What's It Like to Be a Police Officer?* Troll, 1989.

Slater, Teddy. *The Big Book of Real Fire Trucks and Fire-Fighting.* Putnam, 1987.

Bibliography *(cont.)*

People Who Help Us Stay Healthy

Bauer, Judith. *What's It Like to Be a Doctor?* Troll, 1989.

Bauer, Judith. *What's It Like to Be a Nurse?* Troll, 1989.

Behrens, June. *I Can Be a Nurse.* Childrens, 1986.

Berry, Joy W. *Teach Me About the Dentist.* Grolier, 1986.

Braithwaite, Althea. *Visiting the Dentist.* McClanahan, 1990.

Butler, Daphne. *First Look in the Hospital.* Gareth Stevens, 1991.

DeSantis, Kenny. *A Dentist's Tools.* Putnam, 1988.

DeSantis, Kenny. *A Doctor's Tools.* Putnam, 1985.

Drescher, Joan. *Your Doctor, My Doctor.* Walker, 1987.

Elliott, Ingrid G. *Hospital Roadmap: A Book to Help Explain the Hospital Experience to Young Children.* Resources Children, 1984.

Hankin, Rebecca. *I Can Be a Doctor.* Childrens, 1985.

Hautzig, Deborah. *A Visit to the Sesame Street Hospital.* Random House, 1985.

Krall, Charlotte and Judith M. Jim. *Fat Dog's First Visit: A Child's View of the Hospital.* Pritchett & Hull, 1987.

Rogers, Fred. *Going to the Dentist.* Putnam, 1989.

Rogers, Fred. *Going to the Doctor.* Putnam, 1986.

Stamper, Judith. *What's It Like to Be a Dentist?* Troll, 1989.

Watson, Jane W., et al. *My Friend the Doctor: A Read Together Book for Parents and Children.* Crown, 1987.

Other Community Workers

Civardi, Anne. *Things People Do.* EDC, 1986.

Florian, Douglas. *Auto Mechanic.* Greenwillow, 1991.

Florian, Douglas. *People Working.* HarperCollins, 1983.

Hazen, Barbara S. *Mommy's Office.* Macmillan, 1992.

Johnson, Jean. *Postal Workers: A to Z.* Walker, 1987.

Merriam, Eve. *Daddies at Work.* S&S Trade, 1989.

Merriam, Eve. *Mommies at Work.* S&S Trade, 1989.

Moncure, Jane B. *What Can We Play Today?* Childs World, 1987.

Rylant, Cynthia. *Mr. Griggs' Work.* Orchard, 1989.

Stamper, Judith. *What's It Like to Be a Bus Driver?* Troll, 1990.

Thaler, Mike. *What Could a Hippopotamus Be?* Simon & Schuster, 1990.

Records

Beardon, Libby Core, Camille Core Gife, and Kathleen Patrick. *ABC's in Bubbaville.* Kimbo, Inc., 1986.